A Tempered and Humane Economy

A Tempered and Humane Economy

Markets, Families, and Behavioral Economics

Jannett Highfill
Patricia Podd Webber

LEXINGTON BOOKS
Lanham • Boulder • New York • London

Published by Lexington Books
An imprint of The Rowman & Littlefield Publishing Group, Inc.
4501 Forbes Boulevard, Suite 200, Lanham, Maryland 20706
www.rowman.com

Unit A, Whitacre Mews, 26-34 Stannary Street, London SE11 4AB

British Library Cataloguing in Publication Information Available

Library of Congress Cataloging-in-Publication Data

Highfill, Jannett K.
A tempered and humane economy : markets, families, and behavioral economics / Jannett Highfill and Patricia Podd Webber.
pages cm
Includes bibliographical references and index.
ISBN 978-0-7391-9453-9 (cloth : alk. paper) -- ISBN 978-0-7391-9454-6 (electronic)
1. Families. 2. Economics--Psychological aspects. I. Webber, Patricia Podd. II. Title.
HQ503.H54 2015
306.85--dc23
2014043998

∞ ™ The paper used in this publication meets the minimum requirements of American National Standard for Information Sciences Permanence of Paper for Printed Library Materials, ANSI/NISO Z39.48-1992.

Printed in the United States of America

For Karen, Laura, John, Kristina, and KelliAnn

For Donna and Louis Highfill

Contents

I

Each Person, Each Family

Chapter One

The Wisdom of Families

You get up from the Thanksgiving dinner table and drive out in a terrible rain storm to rescue someone, even though you told her just two days ago to get the car battery checked. And she would do it for you. What "family" means depends on circumstances, but for this book that person is family—whether you're technically related or not. And "family" means you help if you can.

The motivating impulse of this book is to use what we have experienced in our relationships with those we love best to inform our aspirations for the larger economy. In the past all too often people lived by one set of rules at home and a completely different set of rules at work. Hopefully at home you get what you need and give what you can; both the abilities and the needs of all family members are respected. But at work the focus must be on meeting the needs of customers if a business is to survive in competitive markets. In the past, this sometimes meant that employees' needs were disregarded, their abilities not fostered or respected. It doesn't have to be that way.

We believe that the economy is in the process of being transformed in ways that foster the integration of market and family principles. The result will be a tempered and humane economy. We also believe that widespread prosperity is an essential feature of an economy anyone would choose to live in; all the historical evidence suggests that markets are necessary for prosperity. But unfortunately, the mere existence of markets does not guarantee that many or most people are prosperous; we need market principles, but we also need something else. Recent changes in the structure of families provide that other ingredient. Modern families emphasize sharing both resources and responsibilities, aspiring to give all family members a voice in important decisions. As young adults mature, form new households, and enter the workforce, they bring with them the expectation that they will be treated with respect at home and at work. The economy most people would prefer to live in incorporates both market and family principles, both market and family discipline, both market and family wisdom.

We describe such an economy as "tempered" because the market and family elements are mixed in satisfying proportions. A couple of analogies may clarify what we mean. We're by no means metallurgists, but think about the relationship of iron to steel. Iron ore is melted using coking coal which adds the carbon to make steel. From one point of view iron and steel are the same thing, but from another they most certainly are not. Iron is too weak for many modern industrial uses. (Modern bridges are steel; iron bridges are Victorian.) Steel is *tempered* iron. Thinking of the economy now, the "iron" in the modern economy is markets. Widespread prosperity is impossible without them. But the "fire" that turns markets into a tempered economy is family wisdom—the things we have learned at home and take into the larger economy, the respect we have for others' abilities and needs, and certain moral principles. To mix metaphors, modern families hold the feet of markets to the fire when they expect the economy to provide their children with rewarding and well-compensated jobs. Just as iron is alloyed with many other elements for specialized steels, a modern functional economy requires many alloys; we will think about these throughout the course of the book. But essentially, the iron of markets and the fire of families create a strong and flexible economy.

"Tempered" also makes us think about Johann Sebastian Bach's *Well-Tempered Clavier*. A clavier is any stringed instrument with a keyboard; "tempered" concerns the tuning, whether it permits the modulation between keys without sounding discordant. A "well-tempered" tuning allows for all the major and minor keys. The *Well-Tempered Clavier* contains a fugue and prelude in each major and minor key to show that a well-tempered tuning system is feasible and desirable. Thinking about the economy, a humane economy must facilitate the needs and aspirations of many different people, those who metaphorically sing in a minor key as well as those who sing only in C major. "Retuning" the economy is possible and sometimes desirable, but it is never easy. Think of the difficulty of tuning a piano as compared to tuning a guitar. According to musicologist Tim Smith and pianist and composer David Korevaar, another of Bach's purposes "was to reveal how modern and progressive composition could be informed by conservative ideas."[1] The goal of this book is to reveal how a modern and progressive economy, consistent with the best principles and aspirations of families, can be informed by market ideas that have been pretty well understood for many decades, conservative ideas in that sense. A well-tempered economy allows the pursuit of rewarding endeavors in every major and minor key: raising children, finding meaningful work, and philanthropic contributions.

Such an economy will be humane; it will allow us to bring our better selves and aspirations with us when we interact with others in any economic arena, large or small. Changes in family structure over the last few decades lead us to cautious optimism about the future of the economy. These changes in families are partly caused by rising standards of living—but they are also partly caused by our gradual incorporation of certain psychological insights into our daily lives. "Tough love," "time out," and "acting out" have entered the lexicon of many families. Behavioral economics is the branch of economics that investigates the economic implications of psychological insights, and thus will help us greatly in our thinking about families and about the larger economy.

A tempered and humane economy finds a balance between market and family principles.

NOTE

1. See the hyperpage on Bach's *Well-Tempered Clavier* by musicologist Tim Smith and pianist and composer David Korevaar: http://jan.ucc.nau.edu/tas3/wtc.html.

Chapter Two

Elana's Family Network

The economy needs to work for persons of all incomes. A humane economy cares about families everywhere along the income distribution, and we can learn a lot from the strategies the less prosperous have developed to help them survive. They live in a world of markets but survive by fostering family networks. That statement may well resonate with people everywhere along the income distribution, but families with similar principles sometimes make quite different decisions. Thinking about that is the work of many chapters, but we begin with our friend Elana who has shared her life story with us.

Elana is the middle of thirteen children, learning early to deal with the pressures of a large family. She graduated from high school, something not managed by most of her siblings. But bare economic survival has been and is an issue for her family. With her own children and grandchildren, brothers and sisters, nieces and nephews, and the extended family, she has seen most of the difficulties life brings, but she also sees how people survive. In her world people cope with the continuing struggle to make ends met by helping each other.

Elana, for example, does not have her own laundry facilities so she takes her washing to her sister's and cleans her sister's house in exchange. Quoting Elana,

> not many of us have cars, so members of the family and friends offer transportation to one another. Sometimes there is gas money but at times there isn't and in the case of the latter we may . . . [give] food from our kitchens or the promise of a payment. . . . If one person should happen to get new furniture (which is rare) they will pass their old furniture to someone in need. The same with other household items, clothes, and other things. Those of us that are fortunate to have low paying jobs are usually not any better off than those without. (personal communication)

For many people in tight circumstances, the wider the network of friends and family the better. Carol Stack found that result in the research she did on survival strategies in a poor inner city community. One of the women in Stack's study said: "You can't get help just by sitting at home. . . . You got to get up and go out and meet people, because the very day you go out, that first person you meet may be the person that can help you get the things you want. . . . But you have to have help from everybody and anybody, so don't turn no one down when they come round for help" (Stack 1974, 32).[1] In a somewhat different context, economists have begun to note that non-cooperative behavior can result in ostracism from the group (Borcherding and Filson 2002). For the less prosperous, that is a severe punishment.

Maintaining and enlarging your network is both important and time consuming. At lunch one day we had a chance to hear this behavior in action. A fast food restaurant employee was working the counter when a friend of hers came to apologize for not picking up their children on time from an after-school activity the day before. What caught our attention was not the content of the conversation, one apologized and explained, the other said no problem. But the conversation took upwards of thirty-five minutes and covered mutual friends, life circumstances, and many other things. There was some tension in the air when it began that seemed dispelled by the end. Clearly the conversation was as much about repairing the relationship and reinforcing the network as it was about one specific incident.

Networking sometimes involves things far more serious than sharing laundry facilities or exchanging child care duties. A housing problem last year resulted in Elana having a younger sister move into her bedroom with her for several months. This year it is Elana's turn to seek help. The owner of the house Elana has been renting has not kept up the mortgage payments and so the bank has foreclosed and she has to move. Four weeks is not much time to find a new home for herself, her daughter, and two grandchildren when schools and transportation are issues.

Since their mother's death the eight of Elana's siblings in the area have worked hard at maintaining their close relationships. For example, they have built a tradition unique to them centered on Mother's Day and Father's Day. On Mother's Day the brothers do the planning and cook for the sisters, and on Father's Day it is the reverse. In addition to the meal there is always a "surprise." One we heard about involved water balloons at the park, this planned by the brothers who somehow "forgot" to warn the sisters not to get too dressed up. The closeness the family has maintained provides not only the loving support Elana needs at this time, but it also increases the number of eyes and ears that might learn about a suitable place for her to relocate.

Another survival mechanism for many low income people is called "income patching," meaning small amounts of income are pieced together from many sources and from more than one member of the household. Lisa Servon

(2002) tells the story of a woman named Lorraine. After struggling for some time to make a living she started a "kitchen table" business providing bookkeeping and other business services for grain farmers. She still qualified for public income assistance, but even so she had to supplement "her public assistance and business income with $800 from selling vegetables from her garden, $800 from helping her parents on their farm, and $500 from painting and wallpapering" (Servon 2002, 186). Income patching relies on the family network to develop contacts and information about income earning opportunities, and in many cases the network is where you put together the team that actually gets a job done, the piano moved or the snow shoveled for instance.

There is a saying commonly found in economics textbooks: "Give a man a fish, you feed him for a day. Teach a man to fish, you feed him for a lifetime." As long as you are not too literal minded about it, that saying is true. The tools (net, line, spear, or boat) and the time investments of both the learner and the teacher all have their analogies in the modern economy. We'll have more to say about investment along the way, but essentially it's the only path to prosperity unless you have a rich uncle to chip in.

When push comes to shove, however, consumption has priority over investment. You cannot let your child starve to invest in education for yourself. Most people would be seriously uncomfortable about short changing a child's nutrition in her first few years in order for the parent to get training for a better job—even understanding that the whole family's prospects would be improved in subsequent years. Malnutrition in babies cannot be compensated for by any amount of improved nutrition later, or even the medical care the increased income in later years could provide. A family without sufficient calories will not invest, and should not.

But now think of a family whose circumstances are a little more promising. Suppose the family has just enough for the children to be healthy and for the parent to get some schooling, say a year at a community college to become a medical technician. Investing is a possibility now, unless, for example, the children's grandmother is in poor health. Whether or not she has helped the family in the past, the grandmother's health might have priority. What about the needs of an aunt who took the children for the summer, or the neighbor who watches the children every day after school and is as close as family? The wider the network the greater the chance that someone will have pressing consumption needs that siphon off funds that might be used for investment.

Stack found evidence of this phenomenon in her study: "In 1971 Magnolia's uncle . . . left an unexpected inheritance . . . to Magnolia and Calvin . . . the first time in their lives that . . . [they] ever had a cash reserve. . . . News of its arrival spread throughout their domestic network. . . .Within a month and a half, all of the money was gone" (Stack 1974, 105–7). Those of us in a situation to commonly have an emergency fund need to reflect a moment. We ask ourselves whether an emergency fund of three months expenses is sufficient, or should it be six months. But there are people who manage with only a few days cash reserve, or none at all, and if they get one they find themselves in a position of fielding requests from many people who have helped them out in the past. Sometimes professional athletes with big contracts buy houses and cars for friends and family—but end up broke after their playing days are over. Lottery winners face the same pressures.

A surprising example of the importance of family networks comes from a gang of drug sellers in Chicago. Steven Levitt and Stephen Dubner report on research into the gang's financial records. "The miscellaneous expenses include[d] . . . the costs associated with a gang member's murder. The gang not only paid for the funeral but often gave a stipend of up to three years' wages to the victim's family." The researcher asked the gang leader why—and got a strongly worded response: "as long as you been with us, you still don't understand that their families is our families. We can't just leave 'em out. We been knowing these folks our whole lives, man, so we grieve when they grieve. You got to respect the family" (Levitt and Dubner 2005, 101).

To summarize briefly, for the less prosperous the basic economic unit for survival is a large family network. For the poor this is good for survival but works against investment. And the wider the network the harder it is to invest. If they do successfully invest, some of the benefits will be disbursed throughout the network, which has a dampening effect on a family's willingness to invest. The wider the network the larger these dampening effects. To be clear, we are by no means arguing that networks are only important on the lower end of the income distribution. Many a Wall Street job was obtained by a quiet word from a family friend in the right ear. But if that same Wall Streeter got an inheritance it is unlikely that he would not be able to use it to pay his child's tuition.

One of the key arguments of this book is that families operate in ways that are profoundly different from the way people operate in a market context. The basic principle of markets is that what you get is directly related to what you contribute—the relevant contribution in this context being measured by how much a stranger is willing to pay for whatever good or service you produce. The shorthand version of this principle is that "reward follows contribution." While the market principle is good and has its uses in the larger economy—for reasons we will discuss at various points—few families believe it is appropriate for them at home. First, getting what you need from your family is *not* a reward; you get what you need because you need it. Thus a person's needs are met because of who he or she is, a family member, rather than what he or she does. Of course it's more complicated than that. It is possible to get thrown out of your family, but that is an extreme case.

To say that families don't use the market principle to decide how family resources are allocated does not imply that a family does not have economic principles. For a somewhat simplistic example, if there are two children in a family and one has a greater need for family resources than the other, perhaps because of some health concerns, then the person with the greater need gets more resources. A similar principle holds for the contributions family members make. If one family member is better able to earn income and another is better able to contribute by caring for someone who is ill, then the family will divide its efforts accordingly. We will use the shorthand formulation "respect abilities, respect needs" to describe the way that families make decisions, calling this the family economic principle, or more often just the family principle.

As suggested by the examples earlier in the chapter, this kind of family decision making requires much communication, negotiation, and good will. We discuss family decision making often in this book, but here we want to clear out of the way two "principles" most modern families reject. The first we will call somewhat facetiously the "bad golden rule": he who has the gold rules. For future reference we'll mention that this rule is nothing like the market principle, because a person can have the gold for a lot of reasons that have nothing to do with contribution. (Section III thinks seriously about this matter.) The second principle rejected by many modern households in the United States is authoritarianism. This is not synonymous with the bad golden rule because authority could be based on something besides income, wealth, or other economic factors. But whatever the source of the authority, over time fewer families have chosen this family structure—a point we will revisit in chapter 7.

Our view is that it is wise and morally appropriate for family members to support each other, make sacrifices for each other. In a family you should contribute what you can: income, housework, contacts, whatever you are able. You should get what you need: food and clothing, emotional support, help with schooling or other investment—bearing in mind other family needs. We understand that not all families operate this way, and probably even those that intend to fall short from time to time. While it is difficult to get direct compelling evidence about a family's goals, economists have certainly found indirect evidence that sometimes our behavior in families is motivated by mercenary concerns: think of how nephews sometimes treat rich uncles.[2] But we would argue that living by a sharing principle is morally appropriate for families anywhere on the income distribution. Extending the reach of the family principle to a network rather than just a nuclear family might also be a moral good, but for the poor it can work against investment because it spreads limited resources thinly over many people.

The economist Glenn Loury argues that family networks can have other negative effects on investment. In an interview on social capital, employment, and discrimination he says:

> You could get stuck with the remnants of history because people are embedded in social networks, the nature of which reflects to some degree the effects of past discrimination. Some communities, because of their historical treatment, are impoverished with respect to the human development resources that people must have access to if they are to succeed in the labor market. I speak here not only of material resources, by the way. Also things like, what do the peer groups hold in esteem? What do people derive social benefits from accomplishing? (Clement 2014, 14)

We will consider these issues quite carefully in later chapters.

We also recognize that since everyone lives in a family and most people work, real life is always a mix of family and market principles. The market principle sometimes leaks into families and the family principle leaks into the workplace. They should, as we will forcefully argue in chapter 5. For now we note that living up to your principles requires that a person live in a disciplined way, but the relationship between principles and discipline is complicated.

NOTES

1. The idea that poor families rely on networks is well established in the sociology literature. Stack's book has upwards of 4000 citations in Google Scholar. For a recent survey of the literature see Kissane and Clampet-Lundquist (2012) and the references therein. There is beginning to be some interest in informal networks in the economics literature; see Borcherding and Filson (2002).

2. One of the most famous examples in economics is a study of bequest motives. Briefly, there is some evidence that people who have bequests to leave to their children are visited more often by those children when they are in a retirement living situation. It appears that that the "elderly rich are . . . more frequently visited than are the elderly poor" (Becker 1991, 12). See also Bernheim, Shleifer, and Summers (1986).

Chapter Three

It's Complicated, Investing in Yourself

Investing in yourself is a complicated decision; actually it's a series of complicated decisions over a significant period of time. Sometimes it's easy to compare the decisions of different people, think that the one who invested was behaving in a disciplined way compared to the one who did not. The goal of this chapter is to use some insights from behavioral economics to help us think this through.[1] We'll learn that there are good reasons to reserve judgment about why others make the investment decisions they do, especially when judging the decisions of those who are in different or more difficult economic circumstances.

Think first of a family which is deciding whether to pay for an adult member to take a class at the local community college. Imagine the class costs $500. Suppose for some reason we could be sure that if she took the class her income next year would go up by $700. In one way of thinking it will cost the family $500 now to get $700 next year. Yes, we understand that in real life returns are not nearly that certain and that most of us discount the future a little, so $700 next year might have same value to us as $630 this year. Even with discounting, the return is 26 percent, so it seems that the right decision is obvious. The family member should take the class, even if the family has to borrow the money to pay the tuition and fees, and even if the interest rate on that borrowing is 20 percent.

But one of the insights of behavioral economics is that the way we frame a decision matters, and changing the frame might well change our opinion of what the right decision is. For this example the question is whether the expenditure of $500 for tuition is thought of as a "cost" or a "loss." In some sense the difference in the terms shouldn't matter; the economic facts are the same. But behavioral economics has found that there is a huge difference in our thinking depending on which term is used (Kahneman 2011, 444–46).

The way the decision has been framed so far, the tuition is a "cost" which the family should subtract from the gain or benefit. Since that number is positive in our example, and since virtually all families value more money as compared to less, then the investment should be made.

Now suppose another family framed the problem a little differently. Suppose this family reasoned that for the $500 in tuition they could have purchased a video game system. People who know a lot more about video games than we do tell us this amount of money would get you a good system and several games. We're taking it for granted that buying the video game is expected to create at least $500 worth of pleasure for the family seriously considering buying it. In this case they might think of the tuition payment as a "loss" (of the benefits of the video game system) and the increase in next year's income as a "gain." The change in language from "cost" to "loss" turns out to matter in most people's thinking. People may be willing to put the same importance on costs and benefits in which case costs can dollar-for-dollar be subtracted from gains for a net gain. But nobody puts the same importance on losses and gains (Kahneman 2011, 282–83).

Think about a game you play, Monopoly or tennis or hearts. Follow this line of thought with us for just a moment; we will soon make the connection to our investment example. Most people love to win and hate to lose, but they dislike losing more than they like winning. Did you watch any of the Olympics from Sochi or London? Do you remember the faces of the silver and bronze medal winners? For monetary gains and losses, many people value losses about twice as much as gains (Kahneman 2011, 284). That means you would be about as unhappy losing $50 as you would be happy gaining $100.

This may be a case of academics taking decades to discover what everyone knows. But the compelling evidence is that comparing gains and losses of the same size, the positive psychological value of the gain is smaller than the negative psychological value of the loss. "When directly compared or weighted against each other, losses loom larger than gains. This asymmetry between the power of positive and negative expectations or experiences has an evolutionary history. Organisms that treat threats as more urgent than opportunities have a better chance to survive and reproduce" (Kahneman 2011, 282).

So now returning to the community college vs. video game decision, if a family views the $500 as a loss, then the increase in income next year, the gain, needed to offset that loss would be $1000.[2] In our story, the gain was considerable, $630, but it wasn't nearly as much as $1000. The family that thinks in terms of losses would buy the video game system.

There are many other aspects of the decision that have to be considered in real life; the gains may be over multiple years, for example, or some gains or losses might not be quantifiable. The larger point is that each family would consider its own decision to be perfectly reasonable and that the other family made a mistake. And each family would be unlikely to understand the other family's reasoning—because verbally "losses" sounds a lot like "costs." There is a sense in which the comparison of these two hypothetical families is comparing apples and oranges. But that is exactly the point—there is more than one plausible way to frame this investment decision. One way of thinking isn't right and the other wrong. No matter how prosperous you are, if you think of costs as losses this analysis suggests that you might well not make investments that people who think the other way would.

One of our colleagues who teaches accounting tells us that she sees something like this in a few of her students. A fifth year of college education gives students the opportunity to take the CPA exam, and over a lifetime, licensing increases an accountant's income on average by over a million dollars. But apparently some students think of that last year's expenses as a cost and some as a loss, because some take the fifth year, and some do not. We don't know whether these students come from essentially the same background in terms of income.

In general, adding differences in income to the mix of costs and losses complicates things in a significant way. Daniel Kahneman argues that for the poor costs are always losses because "there are goods that the poor need and cannot afford. . . . Their problem is that all their choices are between losses" (2011, 298). To the poor, investment cost is the loss of the certain current benefit (the video game) for an as yet unrealized, and therefore uncertain, future benefit. The differing actions taken by accounting students about a fifth year of study remind us that some prosperous individuals may also see costs as losses.

There is another aspect of the investment decision affected by differences in income—the impact of the time lapse between making the investment and getting the payoff. Most people hate waiting. A bird in the hand is worth two in the bush. The more waiting hurts the greater the size the return on the investment needs to be for it to be appealing. But how much hardship the waiting creates might well depend on income. A household where money is tight might consider a year to be an eternity to wait for an investment to pay off. If that same household were in better economic circumstances they might be willing to wait a couple of years for a return on their investment.

There is some evidence from behavioral economics that scarcity itself affects decision making because dealing with scarcity is one of the hardest mental tasks a person must confront—and there is a lot of evidence that when a person has had to think quite hard about a given problem it becomes much harder to do well on subsequent tasks. Cass Sunstein in *The New York Review of Books* (September 26, 2013) pulls an example from Mullainathan and Shafir concerning sugar cane farmers in India: "they do far worse on intelligence tests before a harvest, when they have little money and are preoccupied with how to make ends meet, than after a harvest, when cash is plentiful.

Stunningly, the effect of plentiful cash was equivalent to a nine-to-ten-point boost in IQ." Scarcity of any kind has a deep negative impact on our ability to think; for busy people of any income level time is scarce, and "they may have trouble planning for the long term."[3]

The larger point is that a given person might very well invest in a year's education when resources are not scarce and they are not in the "losses." But that person might not invest in that same schooling, even if the expected payoff from the investment were exactly the same, if at the same time they are experiencing some scarcity. When resources are scarce you are more likely to make a "bad" decision.

So far the community college course investment example does not show how the class might increase the family's income in the future. Suppose it helps you get a better job. Investment is required to get a job, and a person who does not have a job needs to invest appropriately to get one. A plant that has laid off 170 people has created 170 families that need investment. Sometimes not, of course, sometimes a person laid off from Caterpillar gets on at Mitsubishi, but since these people will not be unemployed for long they are not our primary concern. We are thinking about the laid off workers who won't readily get a similar job. Virtually any new job requires some education, information technology skills if you drive a delivery truck to deal with the tracking technologies, design and basic chemistry if you fix hair, specialized skills if you drive a front loader or a combine. Someone has to invest in the laid off workers—the question is who pays for it.

To guide our thinking remember the two views of the economy discussed in the previous chapter. Think of someone who believes that the entire economy operates on the basis of the family principle. Such a person believes that since she needs groceries and rent the economy should provide them, but in her own mind she's not a leech, therefore she essentially believes that she has the right to a job. The basic argument is that if the people who are laid off think that they are entitled to a job they may well resist paying for their own retraining. They may believe that any costs of training involved should be borne by the company that laid them off, or the company that will be hiring them, or perhaps simply society at large. Pat lived in Ohio when the steel mills in Youngstown closed in the early 1980s and she remembers that the papers were full of letters to the editor from angry grandfathers whose fathers and sons had worked in the mills, claiming the companies owed their grandsons jobs as fourth generation steel workers.

From a market principle point of view, this feeling of entitlement seems self-indulgent at best. A person who sees everything from a market point of view will almost by definition understand the connection between her desired job (or business, if she has entrepreneurial leanings) and investment. She may defer marriage or other family responsibilities until she has finished her schooling. Even after she has children she continues to update her investments in herself throughout her career because she knows that her only job security is the skill she can provide an employer.

Although a few people may be as doctrinaire as these two extremes suggest, most people have a more complex view of the world, incorporating both market and family principles. The insight from behavioral economics about the asymmetry in our views of gains and losses is again relevant. Consider an experiment done by Kahneman in which he asked people's opinions about the behavior of the (hypothetical) owner of a copy shop. In the experiment scenario, the major employer in the area had closed and there were many people laid off, although his own copy business was unaffected. The research subjects were asked whether it was fair for him to cut wages. Kahneman discovered that people often had one view for a current employee and a quite different view for a new employee. For a current employee of the shop 83 percent of the sample considered it unfair or very unfair to lower the wage; if that worker quits, however, 73 percent thought it acceptable to pay the new worker less than the previous one. In other words, "the entitlement is personal: the current worker has a right to retain his wage . . . [but] the replacement worker has no entitlement to the previous worker's reference wage" (Kahneman 2011, 307).

In our terms, the evaluators seemed to be applying the family principle in the case of a current worker but applying the market principle in the case of a new worker. The current worker is an individual to whom one has responsibilities that are closer to the responsibilities one has to a family or network member. But a new employee is hired from an impersonal labor market—supposing that there were a number of qualified applicants, any of whom might have been hired—so no personal responsibility is implied. In general, a person has certain entitlements when we believe the family principle is most relevant that they do not have when we believe the market principle is most relevant.

The copy shop of this example was not losing profits—and that is an important part of the story. From Kahneman:

> Our overarching question was whether the opprobrium attached to unfairness imposes constraints on profit seeking. We found that it does. We also found that the moral rules by which the public evaluates what firms may or may not do draw a crucial distinction between losses and gains. . . . The existing wage . . . sets a reference point, which has the nature of an entitlement that must not be infringed. It is considered unfair for the firm to impose losses on . . . workers relative to the reference transaction, unless it must do so to protect its own entitlement. (2011, 306)

The firm's entitlement is to "retain its current profit. If it faces a threat of a loss, it is allowed to transfer the loss to others. A substantial majority of respondents believed that it is not unfair for a firm to reduce its workers' wages when its profitability is falling" (Kahneman 2011, 307). The workers' jobs depend on the business continuing to exist.

For another example, think about the currently ballooning deficits of city and state governments that are caused by medical and retirement costs that were negotiated in relatively good economic conditions. The question is whether it is fair to renegotiate in an economic downturn.[4] As Kahneman notes, "negotiations over a shrinking pie are especially difficult, because they require an allocation of losses. People tend to be much more easygoing when they bargain over an expanding pie" (Kahneman 2011, 304).

We also need to emphasize a feeling of entitlement is not necessarily good or bad. People at all income levels have an entitlement mentality about some things at some times. Malcolm Gladwell argues, in fact, that an appropriate sense of entitlement is one of the primary gifts middle and upper income families give their children that lower income children don't necessarily receive (Gladwell 2008, 104–8). Children should be taught, for example, that they are entitled to reasonable answers to their questions from doctors or teachers. It would be great if children of all incomes knew that they were entitled to a sound education and could just rely on their teachers and the educational system to provide access to it for them.

Bluntly, if an inappropriate sense of entitlement sometimes leads people to under-invest because they expect others will take care of them, an appropriate sense of entitlement leads them to make investments because they expect, for example, to get a great education from the investment. Every family at whatever income level needs to conceptualize for their children the difference between an inappropriate sense of entitlement and an appropriate one. A larger point is that people apply the family principle at times and the market principle at other times. Appropriate versus inappropriate entitlement is certainly an area that needs more scientific investigation. Given that society's views of a person's entitlements are complex, it is easy to understand why we sometimes disagree about them. That is one reason we think about democracy in later chapters.

We have relied primarily on insights from behavioral economics in this chapter. The basic idea is that loss aversion, entitlement, and framing—all ideas from behavioral economics—affect our decisions to invest in ourselves. This is true for persons of all income levels—but unfortunately these ideas sometimes work against investment by the poor.

Having raised the question of whether society should invest in those who do not invest enough in themselves, and how collective decisions should be made, we have implicitly raised some significant moral questions. We believe we should state our moral views as forthrightly as possible, so we turn to that in the next chapter.

NOTES

1. Behavioral economics is a large and growing field in economics, taking in many areas of study but we might suggest the three "big ideas" of Laibson (2010, 131) as a first definition of the field. These are (1) "bounded rationality," largely what we will call cognitive biases, (2) "limits to willpower or self-control problems or, more formally, dynamic inconsistency," and (3) that "we care about more than just ourselves and our families." We care about "process," "equity," and "fairness."

2. This calculation uses the principle mentioned above that gains have about half the value of losses.

3. The passage continues: "The cash-poor and the time-poor have much in common with lonely people, for whom relationships with others are scarce. When people struggle with scarcity, their minds are intensely occupied, even taken over, by what they lack" (Sunstein, *The New York Review of Books*, September 26, 2013).

4. In Illinois such renegotiations may even be unconstitutional.

Chapter Four

"It's Not Fair"

"It's not fair!"

"It's fair, John."

"It's not fair!"

"It's fair, John."

Back and forth it went for some time before Nana just gave up and didn't answer. The conversation came about because Pat and granddaughter Laura had been morning zoo volunteers. They were in the habit of stopping at the ice cream stand after working at the zoo to get Laura a mini cone to tide her over until lunch was ready, but that day Papa had brought her brother John to visit the zoo, so he was going home with the girls. The children noticed a McDonalds across the street from the ice cream stand, and the children wanted to have lunch there before they got ice cream. Nana agreed, but with the strict stipulation that there would be no ice cream unless they finished their lunch, the rule at home. You can probably figure out which child didn't.

You might say this is an example of trying to help the children learn about both market discipline, the reward of ice cream follows the contribution of mucking camel stalls, and family discipline, you get the lunch you need, but an ice cream treat depends on abiding by family rules teaching the importance of individual responsibility. There's something about grand-parenting that forcefully reminds us of the moral foundations of most economic choices, including ice cream. "It's not fair" is a close cousin of "It's not right."

To start with the most basic moral responsibility regarding economic matters, anyone who is not disabled must support himself and his minor children.[1] When growing up our friend Lois used to hear her mother say that "work is the rent you pay for the space you occupy on this earth." The corollary is that it is not anyone else's moral responsibility to support us or our children under normal circumstances. It is society's moral responsibility to provide an economy in which we can meet our personal moral responsibilities. Both individuals and society have responsibilities in this regard: working out the conditions and qualifications of them is a major focus of this book.

In our view your second responsibility is to recognize that, although your ability to work and earn income depends on your personal talents and efforts, it also depends on your education, background, opportunities, and many other things over which you had little control. Peter Singer (whom we will discuss further in just a moment) cites Herbert Simon's estimate that as much as 90 percent of earnings are produced by "social capital" as compared to a person's own activity (Singer 2009, 26). Social capital includes such things as the legal system, the transportation system, the education system, the banking system, as well as the moral fiber of society (Colander 2013, 604). Social capital also includes social norms that foster cooperation and trust, which have been shown to have "substantial effects on economic growth" and economic welfare in the long run (quotation is from Borcherding and Filson 2002; evidence is from Zak and Knack 2001). We take social capital so much for granted we hardly realize how important it is for the way we live.

For sufficiently prosperous individuals who are able to live by the first two principles, we propose a third moral responsibility—to work in a field that makes a contribution to human kind. If you work for a firm that makes earth moving equipment, for example, you should believe that moving dirt contributes to the betterment of human kind, perhaps by building a road, or digging the foundation for a home or a hospital.

These do not exhaust a person's important economic responsibilities, of course. The Arts and Crafts movement associated with William Morris and John Ruskin would have said that there is a moral obligation on buyers to buy conscientiously and well. Distinguishing between enlightened self-interest and greed is also necessary. To correct the famous movie *Wall Street*, greed is *not* good.

Greed is defined by the influential moral philosopher Mortimer Adler as "the wrong desire for more houses than one can put to use, more shoes than one can wear, more food than one can eat and remain healthy" (Adler 1991, 48). But the application of this moral principle in a modern monetized economy is not at all simple. As Adler admits, it is no simple task to calculate how much money a person needs for future necessities. You do not know how long you will live and how much medical care you will need to pay for, and thus how much of your income you need to prudently set aside for yourself.

Another moral necessity is that equals be treated equally. The modern statement of this principle is by Amartya Sen. Any viable ethical system requires an equality of something among persons, the question being equality of what. Among the economic possibilities are income, wealth, opportunity, and well-being (Sen 1995, ix).[2] Given that persons are different in many ways, Sen also recognizes that equality in any one thing will result in inequality in many other things. For a simple example, you can make everyone pay the same dollar amount for a given tax, or the same percentage of their income, but not both. For our purposes perhaps the most important application of this rule is that there should be equality of opportunity. That is, all persons should live under the same rules and have access to the same opportunities to invest in themselves, especially to educate themselves. We believe most Americans agree with this idea. Chapters 11 and 22 return to some issues in making it operational.

Before we think further about our personal moral responsibilities, we want to mention that many religious traditions advocate a preferential regard for the poor—regardless of whether you live in (or would prefer to live in) a humane, market, socialist, or traditional economy.[3] We could say the same for many philosophical schools and traditions. We will take two contemporary philosophers as representative of current thinking about the necessity of systematic redistribution to help the poor. Peter Singer (2009) and Garrett Cullity (2004) have argued that redistribution, above and beyond what we do automatically by paying taxes, is a moral responsibility for all who can afford it. The basic argument is that one person should not have a luxury if anyone else is lacking a necessity. Singer argues that "suffering and death from lack of food, shelter, and medical care are bad. . . . If it is in your power to prevent something bad from happening, without sacrificing anything nearly as important, it is wrong not to do so" (Singer 2009, 15). Later Singer adds

> No principle of obligation is going to be widely accepted unless it recognizes that parents will and should love their own children more than the children of strangers, and, for that reason, will meet the basic needs of their children before they meet the needs of strangers. But this doesn't mean that parents are justified in providing luxuries for their children ahead of the basic needs of others. (Singer 2009, 139)

So does basic morality really require this high degree of redistribution? This is something we need to think about.

It's Sunday afternoon and we've set aside some time to ponder the depth of our responsibilities to the poor. The operational question for us this afternoon is whether to spend a few dollars for ice cream or donate that money to an aid agency, say Dress for Success that helps people prepare for job interviews. Singer bluntly says that we rich Americans spend a lot of money on things we don't need—money that should go to alleviate the suffering of the poor (Singer 2009, 11–12).

Would anyone argue that ice cream is more important than alleviating suffering? Surely a person would be immoral to choose an ice cream cone over a contribution to a charity. But you can have the ice cream and still donate to charity, just not as much. Pleasure and enjoyment are a part of a good life, and there is wisdom in getting pleasure from small things. Peppermint ice cream with chocolate sauce.

So we'd argue that the interesting question is how much ice cream as compared to how large a contribution to charity. A person who donates a penny to an appropriate charity would hardly have satisfied the moral demands on him or her. Likewise a person who chooses ice cream from time to time is not doing wrong, even though he or she understands that the money spent on the ice cream, when donated to an appropriate charity, might help relieve the suffering of another.

We truly believe our jobs are either the best or among the best chances we have for making the world a better place. We chose teaching over medical school or physics. We are among the many people who became economists at least partly in order to understand poverty and help others do the same.[4] As much as we get great satisfaction and enjoyment from time in the classroom, our job has quite a few aspects that no one could possibly enjoy. The latter are time-consuming, tedious, boring—and persuading yourself to do them is not easy. Spending Sunday afternoon at the office recording grades or filling out paperwork does not replace a walk in the park.

So the issue is what provides a person the incentive to work hard and smart. The more you earn the more you can give. And frankly, promising ourselves some ice cream later does a better job bribing us to come in and get some work done than promising that we'll make a contribution to charity.

Finally, odd as it seems to economists, we want to acknowledge that there are serious thinkers who believe that prosperity per se is immoral. In chapter 16 we will give examples of individuals led down immoral paths by the pursuit of prosperity. A similar idea, but less extreme, is that some prosperity is good, but that increases in prosperity are not always good. Some economists have begun to make the argument that for people in the middle to upper reaches of the income distribution an increase in income often leads to less happiness rather than more and is therefore morally inappropriate (Bruni 2012, 94). The higher income, for example, may require a high time commitment; earning it may be stressful and hard on family relationships. The temptation to spend money on frivolities may be too great. You may have enough money to indulge in activities that turn into life destroying addictions.

Granting this argument for a moment, we believe per capita GDP in the United States is less than the optimal level of prosperity. Some non-economists are even willing to put a dollar value on the amount of income that maximizes happiness, around $75,000 (Gladwell 2013, 52). We're not sure about their methodology but we are sure per capita GDP in the United States, at just under $53,000 in 2013, does not approach that number. An increase in average prosperity would make people happier; it would certainly help people in Elana's neighborhood. Although prosperity sometimes creates its own moral challenges, ultimately in this book we come down on the side that prosperity is good and that increases in prosperity are good.

Steven Pinker even makes the argument that the increasing prosperity of market economies is the cause of the decline in violence from the mid-twentieth century to the present in the developed world, and that markets contributed more than democracy per se (Pinker 2012, 288).[5] The reason may be related to the change in human thinking required by mutually agreed upon exchange rather than tradition or coercion. It has been argued that in thinking about what might appeal to a buyer, cinnamon bread versus rye bread for example, the baker imagines the point of view of the buyer. Even such a pragmatic consideration may be one step on the path toward developing empathy for the buyer. Pinker reminds us that actions matter; empathy sets off "epiphanies of concern for members of overlooked groups [but] . . . for empathy to matter, it must goad changes in policies and norms" (Pinker 2012, 591). More recently, one of the signal accomplishments of the twentieth century has been the development of human rights as a commitment that all human beings "no matter how distant . . . be safe from harm and exploitation" (Pinker 2012, 591). Prosperity has profound non-economic benefits. Later we will argue that increases in prosperity can be expected to increase other moral goods.

NOTES

1. The treatment of disabled persons in a tempered and humane economy is an enormously important topic in its own right; one that would require another book to begin to do it justice.

2. Notice that he does not mention "happiness" or desire fulfillment as the thing to be equalized especially for people in a situation of "entrenched inequalities and deprivations" because they might not even entertain the idea of some enjoyable things if they know they couldn't possibly afford them (Sen 1995, 55). He thus rejects the idea of keeping people happy by keeping them poor.

3. Buddha taught a version of the Golden Rule, emphasizing that true charity means giving while expecting nothing in return. Moses taught "Love your neighbor as yourself"; the gleaning laws required landowners to leave the edges of the fields for the poor, for example. In Islam all wealth is considered as a gift from God, meant to be shared through the Third Pillar of Islam, Zakat, or compulsory charity. In the sayings of Laozi, founder of Taoism, "To practice virtue is to selflessly offer assistance to others, giving without limitation one's time, abilities, and possessions in service, whenever and wherever needed, without prejudice concerning the identity of those in need." Jesus tells a rich young man to sell all his possessions and give the money to the poor. The Coptic Christian Shenoute asks, "Will our heart be able to take in love for the neighbor when we have not first emptied it of love for money . . . ?" Please see Shenoute's *Athanasius: The Life of Antony* translated by Robert C. Gregg, 1980.

4. As did many economists, Alfred Marshal, John Maynard Keynes, Joan Robinson, and Paul Samuelson, to only get started. Those interested in a readable treatment of the history of economics might see Nasar (2011). Röpke (1986) has an interesting theoretical treatment of the appropriate integration of government and market, focusing essentially on the European econo-

my. The analysis is perhaps a bit dated now but does articulate his vision of a humane economy.

5. If you are skeptical that violence in the world has indeed declined, please read his book for the evidence before you make up your mind on the question.

Chapter Five

Talk the Walk

In the previous chapter we thought about some of our primary moral responsibilities relating to economic matters. Here we want to extend our thinking in one important way. In chapter 2 we characterized the market principle as economic reward follows economic contribution, and the family principle as "respect abilities, respect needs." Much of the work of this book will be to think about how the economy should incorporate both ideas in appropriate ways. But to do that, each person, each family must get the mix of principles right a substantial proportion of the time. Becoming such a person is one of the great human tasks, of the same importance and gravity as pursuing the highest creative or spiritual disciplines.

The essential problem is that the evidence from behavioral economics suggests that we quickly classify situations as either market or family, often without being aware of it, and behave quite differently depending on these classifications. Our first reactions can be quite dichotomous. As Dan Ariely reports:

> A few years ago . . . the AARP asked some lawyers if they would offer less expensive services to needy retirees, at something like $30 an hour. The lawyers said no. Then the program manager from AARP had a brilliant idea: he asked the lawyers if they would offer free services to needy retirees. Overwhelmingly, the lawyers said yes. . . . When money was mentioned, the lawyers used market norms and found the offer lacking, relative to their market salary. When no money was mentioned they used social norms and were willing to volunteer their time. (Ariely 2008, 71)

Ariely's view is that people should be cautious about triggering market norms in other people's thinking. Our view is that everyone must find the appropriate balance between market and family norms (social norms in Ariely's terminology). Doing so is sufficiently difficult that it requires a conscious deliberate effort. It is learned behavior. We'll mention a couple of encouraging examples, and then mention one that is more problematic.

Jannett has a friend who is in the Human Resources division of a major corporation. Recently she was in the position of having to permanently dismiss an employee. As it happened that employee was a relatively new engineer still in the probationary period. He had a great skill set but it did not match up well with the needs of the firm, so firing him was a market transaction. Even though the employee was fired, the firm offered him some help with the transition to his next employment. His separation package included job coaching, advice on resume writing, and the like. You could argue that the firm was just protecting itself legally, or trying to prove it was a good employer to facilitate future hiring. But we'd argue that they were showing attention to his needs as a human being as well. These explanations are not mutually exclusive. It might well be that the family principle was being respected. When the shoe is on the other foot sometimes a person who is quitting a job trains a replacement or writes up some helpful strategies or procedures for the next person in the job—just from a desire to help those real human beings who have to get the work done in the future.

Pat has a friend whose grandchild needs a particular kind of physical therapy where an adult family member must help, but to do so the child has to hold his leg in a certain way. The grandmother invented a specific sling to assist in that. Later it occurred to her that children with the same medical condition all across the country have the same need, and would benefit from the same sling. She is in the process of starting a company to make and sell the sling. Her primary motive is to help children, but the activity must at least pay for itself because she isn't in a position to put a large amount of family resources into the endeavor for an indefinite period of time.

It seems to us that this is a great example of a situation that requires an adroit mix of family and market principles. On the one hand, no one chooses a health situation for a family member, so the grandmother's initial invention certainly reflects the family principle. But she did choose to try to market the item to others. The people she's hoping to help didn't choose to be in their situation either. But they will buy her product only if they choose. Succeeding will require a considerable facility with market reasoning. In fact, we might argue that many businesses were started essentially this way—by people earning their living satisfying an important need. There's nothing that says an enterprise begun as a reflection of the family principle can't end up doing more good by embracing the market principle in appropriate ways. In chapter 21 we will argue that is a path that helps both the individual and society at large.

Finding the right balance can be quite difficult. Jannett had a friend who successfully ran a small business (about $5 million in revenue) for many years. He understood the market principle pretty well—and that one part of running a business is treating your employees with courtesy and respect if you want to keep them. So he took his frustrations out on his understanding wife at home. Later in life after his wife died he moved to an assisted living facility where he barked at the staff everyday just as he had at his wife at home—treating them like family so to speak. But the management of the facility had to deal with the fact that to the employees it was a market situation because they had other job options. After the man ignored repeated warnings he was moved to a restricted wing where he had fewer freedoms. Misunderstanding the relative application of family discipline as compared to market discipline can sometimes have profound consequences as it did in this case.

As these examples suggest, many situations are complex, and we need to give both market and family principles their due. We reject on moral grounds the possibility of deciding economic questions by violence or coercion. Nor is tradition acceptable if it tolerates prejudicial attitudes or violates basic human rights. There is a moral imperative to get the mix of family and market principles about right. If you habitually err on the side of thinking of situations as being "family" when they are "market," then you may depend on others when you should depend on yourself. On the other hand, if you always simplistically think in market terms you may break the basic moral principle of never using any person as a means to an end. [1]

We titled this chapter "Talk the Walk." For us Walking the Walk is achieving the appropriate balance of market and family principles. We've noticed that some of our colleagues in economics seem to talk as if they believe only in the market principle. Sometimes they even teach that way. But when you work with them on a daily basis, or serve on a committee with them trying to accomplish important goals, their behavior is much wiser than their talk. They balance market wisdom and family wisdom. Usually we say that people should "Walk the Talk" to suggest that they should change their actions so it matches their talk. But here we would like to gently suggest that they consider revising their talk to match their actions. Keep the walk, change the talk, because after all someone might be listening.

No one is exempt from the task of finding balance. But we call out ourselves, economists, in particular. We understand markets need a moral defense, but in the process of providing one sometimes we go a touch too far in our rhetoric. No one could keep a family together if you actually tried to live as if market rules always rule.

NOTE

1. While this is hardly the place to discuss Kantian ethics, a common statement of this principle is from *Groundwork of the Metaphysic of Morals*: "Act in such a way that you treat humanity, whether in your own person or the person of any other, never merely as a means to an end, but always at the same time as an end."

Chapter Six

What's Luck Got To Do With It?

Quite a lot actually. Luck is often involved in business success, and it certainly affects investment. Talent and hard work pay off best by being in the right place at the right time.[1] The furniture store Pat's maternal grandfather owned was liquidated at 1928 prices rather than at the much lower ones that prevailed for many years following the crash of 1929, and her family had a better financial head start because of it. Our focus being on prosperity and investment, luck affects people in ways that are not always obvious.

A study was made at the National Bureau of Economic Research on the effects of the No Child Left Behind Act. The Act stipulated that in cases where schools failed to meet the standards for two consecutive years parents would be allowed to choose another school for their children. In the Charlotte-Mecklenburg NC School District there were not enough openings in the better schools for all the children whose parents wanted to move them, so a lottery was held to decide which children would be accommodated. Researchers Justine Hastings and Jeffrey Weinstein found that students who won the lottery were less likely to be suspended and had higher test scores than the ones who lost (Hastings and Weinstein 2008). In a similar case in New York, children selected for a magnet school by lottery from "the housing projects and bodegas of West Harlem and Washington Heights" showed similar improvements (Tough 2012, 88). There is no more pure example of luck than a lottery, and here it affected children's education, that is, their income earning ability for the rest of their lives. We have to be honest and say that other researchers have not found any correlation between winning the lottery for a good school and future educational outcomes (Levitt and Dubner 2005, 158–59). We will spend considerable time in chapter 11 talking about what seems to matter for education. For now, we will stick with the matter of luck, and consider a rather clear cut example of how luck affects children.

Take children starting school for the first time. There must be a cut-off date. Children born before a certain date start this year, those born after that date start next year. What that means is that just by the intersection of policy and luck, some children are almost a year older than others in a given grade. That might not matter much except that in most places we start doing "ability grouping" at a very young age. As often as not, for very young children, those differences in ability start out as differences in age. Six or nine months mean a lot to the development of a six year old. And the child who is identified as being of high ability receives more encouragement and opportunities to learn than a child of average or low ability. Performance is cumulative, and the effects of the policy can be long lasting. There is evidence that the difference in performance between the youngest and the oldest members of a class persists all the way into college (Gladwell 2008, 27–30).

That luck matters is hardly a controversial idea. The harder problem is making judgments about how much of a role luck has played in a given outcome as compared to other factors. The heart-breaking thing about the differences in lifelong performance based on whether your birthday is August or September is that it's relatively easy to design policies to fix the problem, such as having classes where the maximum difference in ages is three months for the younger grades for example. But you can't fix a problem you haven't seen and acknowledged.

At the coffee hour after Sunday School Jannett overheard a man telling some others about a church member who was fifty-three years old, obese, and had been on welfare all her adult life. One person expressed sympathy, thinking that there must be some underlying health issue. Another essentially said she was lazy; she should lose weight and get a job. The third said the woman's full time job was figuring out ways to milk the welfare system. As near as Jannett could tell, none of the bystanders knew this woman personally. A key insight from behavioral economics is that these commentators were doing what everyone would and must do.

> You cannot help dealing with the limited information you have as if it were all there is to know. You build the best possible story from the information available to you, and if it is a good story you believe it. Paradoxically, it is easier to construct a coherent story when you know little, when there are fewer pieces to fit into the puzzle. Our comforting conviction that the world makes sense rests on a secure foundation: our almost unlimited ability to ignore our ignorance. (Kahneman 2011, 201)

Each of these commentators may have had some personal association pop into their mind that caused them to jump to the conclusion they did. Possibly the first knows people whose health prevented them from working. The second may have a lazy brother-in-law. And the third may have recently read a story about a welfare cheat. "Associative thinking" is one of the ways our brain makes short and easy work of something we don't want to take the time and energy to think about. Although the fact may make us uncomfortable, the evidence is that associative thinking is done unconsciously, that is, without our being aware of the triggering idea.

Now suppose the church members were called upon to help this woman in some way. Which speaker do you think would help? And the reasons for the decisions made may be subconscious, the individuals being completely unaware of why they have made a particular judgment call. The behavioral economists call these mental glitches "cognitive biases."

Our judgment of the woman's situation is influenced by how often we have heard similar stories, and oddly, only part of the story needs to be familiar for it to feel true (Kahneman 2011, 62). So if you have heard the poor health story often, but rarely heard the welfare cheat explanation, you are much more likely to believe the former. Again somewhat oddly, the happenstance order of the comments overheard makes a difference in our judgment. If our brain is busy with the first "story" we have to "unbelieve" it before we can give the second story brain time, as it were (Kahneman 2011, 81). First impressions are important in more situations than in job interviews and when meeting new people.

What makes this even more problematic is that when our (unconscious) mental processes cause us to have a biased view, we are just as confident in our conclusion as we would be if we had thought much harder. "Neither the quantity nor the quality of the evidence counts for much in subjective confidence. The confidence that individuals have in their beliefs depends mostly on the quality of the story. . . . We often fail to allow for the possibility that evidence that should be critical to our judgment is missing" (Kahneman 2011, 87). If you have decided that this woman's situation is caused by an underlying health condition, you will be quite confident that you are correct.

Everyone makes these mistakes in thinking called cognitive biases. We are not exempt. No one is. Jannett is much too quick to jump to conclusions; Pat is overly practical. Let's look now at three more specific biases that may lead to mistakes in judgment.

Think of how a church member might hear about welfare abuse. When a particularly flagrant abuse of the welfare system makes the local news, a group like the Associated Press picks it up and passes it on through radio and TV; in this day it's destined for the blogosphere. We forget that it is news precisely because of its novelty. A story you've heard recently pops into your subconscious easily, making it seem more frequent than it is. We react to it, and as Kahneman says, the "emotional tail wags the rational dog" (Kahneman 2011, 140).

Often we look at results and assign causes. Have you ever caught yourself "Monday morning quarterbacking"? On Monday you know the pass was going to be intercepted so you never would have called that play. The essential problem is that we tend to equate good outcomes with good decisions. Suppose you are thinking of starting a business that has a 50 percent chance of survival—but if it did your lifetime income would triple or quadruple. Starting the business is the right decision, *even* if it fails. A person who later says you made a bad decision because the business has failed is wrong; perhaps the critic has forgotten that timing, lucky or unlucky, is often critical in investment results.

Even worse, we forget that we would have done (and should have done) the exact same thing under the same circumstances. "A general limitation of the human mind is its imperfect ability to reconstruct past states of knowledge, or beliefs that have changed" (Kahneman 2011, 202). Our minds seem to protect themselves by forgetting that we have ever changed our minds about something.

The punch line is that these biases lead us to be unintentionally harsh in our judgments about people, especially those in difficult economic circumstances. We tend to assign good decision making to prosperous people and bad decision making to the poor. We identify with the rich, in that we by and large see ourselves as having made good decisions. As for the poor, we often look for what they did wrong, ignoring things like health, educational opportunities, family circumstances and pressures, and pure luck. One goal of this chapter has been to use the insights from behavioral economics about cognitive biases to help us develop a more nuanced view of the role that luck plays in economic life. Chapter 16 will particularly draw on this insight.

One last cognitive bias, the "optimism bias," deserves a mention. When proposing a project business executives tend to overestimate benefits and underestimate costs—so do the leaders of governments and non-governmental organizations (NGOs) or no one would fund them (Kahneman 2011, 256-57). If the poor start few businesses it may be that they are simply being realistic, that they read the costs and benefits well enough to know when the decks are stacked against them.

We are now ready to collect our thoughts about what economic discipline means for the individual. It means having principles and living up to them. We have framed these as the family principle, "respect abilities, respect needs" and the market principle that economic reward follows economic contribution. When they conflict, we have to find a path forward that gives full weight to both and that does not violate our basic moral responsibilities: to support oneself, to be mindful of the help of others, and to do meaningful work. Investment particularly requires economic discipline, but our insights from behavioral economics help us understand that the converse—that noninvestors are undisciplined—does not follow. The interactions between risk aversion and framing, the effects of scarcity, the nuances of appropriate and inappropriate entitlement—even a cursory understanding of these suggests that investment, especially for the poor, is much more than a question of whether or not a person exercises self-discipline.

The cognitive biases of this chapter affect our self-discipline in a different way. By and large our brains operate in ways that we are only dimly aware of if we notice them at all. So even when we have made a particular decision, to attend a certain class for example, cognitive biases all too often create a gap between setting the goal and achieving it. In setting a particular goal we might have told ourselves a story about the situation that oversold the benefits and underestimated the difficulties, or for that matter ignored the ever present implications of luck and timing. No amount of discipline, economic or otherwise, takes away these cognitive biases—they are "hard-wired." There will always be at least a momentary gap between good intentions and good behavior—as everyone on a diet can attest.

Prosperity and everything good that comes with it is impossible without economic discipline, but most individuals need considerable help from time to time navigating through the process of creating prosperity. We have essentially two things to help us, our families and certain aspects of the larger economy, both of which temper our view of the possibilities. The next chapter begins our thinking about how our families help us personally, and provides some guidance to our thinking about the larger economy.

NOTE

1. You've used the ubiquitous Post-It Notes. The adhesive was developed by Spencer Silver at 3M in 1968, but it wasn't until 1974 when his colleague Art Fry put some on his bookmark to make it both moveable and sticky that the sticky notes were born. Read the story in Henry Petroski's 1994 book *The Evolution of Useful Things*. Many other examples can be found in Gladwell (2008).

Chapter Seven

The Wisdom of Families—Supporting Each Other's Decisions

We began this section with an argument that the wisdom of families is an essential element of a tempered and humane economy. We want to end with some reflections on how families operate at their best, noting some encouraging changes over time. Suppose that right now a family faces a significant economic decision. Every family member has mulled it over, and gathered whatever information he or she feels is necessary. It's time for a family meeting. Carolyn Heilbrun defines "power" as "the ability to take one's place in whatever discourse is essential to action and the right to have one's part matter" (Heilbrun 1988, 18). Hopefully everyone in the family feels "empowered"—entitled to have their say in the conversation. Family brainstorming may help you arrive at a solution better than any individual would have thought of. But even if that doesn't happen, if you truly feel that other family members have heard you, understand how you think and what you feel, then you will be able to live with the solution arrived at, even if you would not have chosen it yourself. In a functional family, everyone's ideas, needs, and contributions are respected, and in that sense everyone is treated as an equal.

We have referred to the family principle as "respect abilities, respect needs" to emphasize the inter-relationships among all family members. It seems to us that in the United States this concept of a functional family has been gaining ground only since about World War II. When the pattern in families was that the father was the breadwinner, the father was the decision maker. Until 1980 there was even a "head of the household" designation on census forms. The petty kitchen tyrant (male or female) no doubt still exists, but that is less consistent with society's ideas about how things should be.

In the language of modern psychology, modern families rarely have an authoritarian structure, and choose either equality matching or communal sharing as their organizing principle (Pinker 2012, 631–32).[1] Equality matching is when household members take turns, keep track of chores done or money spent, know what needs to be done to have everyone's efforts and rewards balance out. In communal sharing the idea is that family members get just as much enjoyment from another family member's success as they do from their own, so that it doesn't matter who does a chore as long as it gets done (Pinker 2012, 631–32).[2] In practice families mix and match between these structures, but the authoritarian pattern is not the default structure.

In the last section of the book we will argue that these historically new family practices are a reason to believe the economy will improve over time. Here we want to focus on another particularly important aspect of what it means to be a member of a functional family. These families recognize the value of each member being able to make important decisions for himself or herself, and of having their family's support in doing so. However, what we've learned about cognitive biases suggests that everyone's point of view needs a little adjustment from time to time. Families often see mistakes in thinking more quickly than the individual does, and they can help. They work quite hard at communication, expressing feelings and brainstorming solutions. Functional families try quite hard to support each other's decisions.

Families also recognize that to not have choices is to be impoverished in a significant sense.[3] Your choices determine your life: how to best pursue those things that give life its meaning, whether and whom to marry, whether to follow a particular spiritual discipline, or which artistic area to cultivate. One especially important decision concerns what you do to provide economic support for the family. Looking for a new job is often time consuming, expensive, and stressful. This is where prosperity matters, and truthfully, how supportive a family can be of the decisions of a family member does depend on the family's prosperity. It's difficult or impossible to support a decision to look for a new job if it means leaving a job that the family relies on for rent money, due tomorrow.

As much as we regret it, there is an implication in this fact for less prosperous people that has to be mentioned. We sometimes hear it said that the working poor, especially those who work full time, are poor because they are not paid what they are worth. This raises the question of how to know what a person's work is worth. That's a difficult question, but the only way to know for sure is to test the job market.[4] But a family's prosperity has everything to do with that being a realistic option. The poorer you are the more likely it is that you are not being paid your worth, other things being equal, because looking for that new job is a choice you're less likely to have. Our friend Elana has been in that situation. Simply having choices is a measure of prosperity; the more prosperous you are the more choices you have.

To close this section, a functional family gives us a foundation to help each of us cope with our cognitive biases and bad luck. A functional family also understands it lives and works in the context of a larger economy—and that an economy is like a family in some ways, but nothing like a family in others. We now turn our attention to these macro issues.

NOTES

1. For Pinker this change in households is one of the many "beneficial consequences of an application of reason to human affairs" (2012, 690). It is an extension of the ideas and consequences of the enlightenment: "receptiveness to cooperation, democracy, classical liberalism, and nonviolence" (2012, 692). We would add prosperity to the list.

2. Pinker also points out that this often results in wives feeling they get a larger proportion of the work and a smaller proportion of the appreciation.

3. We're thinking here of situations with a relatively small number of choices. Having two choices is better than one, three better than two. But behavioral economics has helped us recognize that it is possible to have too many choices. For example, there is good evidence that having fewer choices for Medicare Part D, the prescription drug part of the program, would improve decision making for many people (Hough 2013, 93–94).

4. Sometimes the question of what a given job is worth can be answered by appropriate statistical comparisons of job categories. When this information is available it should be used. But often that is only a partial answer and frequently it's no help whatsoever. Unless your employer has recently hired someone for essentially the same job, the only way to know what your labor is worth is to go job hunting. The answer to the question always depends on the economic context, where you live most particularly. So the bottom line is, you think you're worth a million dollars a year? Persuade someone to pay you that and we'll believe you.

II

The Big Picture: Investment Decisions in Context

Chapter Eight

The Wisdom of Families—Democracy Is Learned at Home

One of the crucial ideas we bring forward from the first section is that creating prosperity is an important goal of a macroeconomy. We recognize that each person's prosperity depends in great part on family decisions. But now we want to shift our attention to the other side of the equation. Yes, what you and your family are able to do matters enormously. But all prosperous persons have had significant investments made in them by the larger community—by people who are not a part of their personal family network by any stretch, by strangers. Any time our prosperity depends on the decisions made by other people, conflicts arise. When a large number of people who don't know each other are involved, the only solution is to vote, the essence of our democratic social contract. For example, what a parent can do for his child's education may well depend on taxpayers' willingness to spend on schools or scholarship programs.

Understanding that brings us squarely to questions of democracy in action. As a very small child Jannett remembers her grandmother teaching her that taxes are the price we pay to live in a democracy. As she got a bit older her grandmother would make the analogy to a church or service organization or charity—completely voluntary organizations. If you're a member of one of these for any period of time issues will come up where reasonable people disagree. Jannett's grandmother was famous for making a strong, cogent argument for the approach she thought best, but at the end of the day if she lost the vote—well, she paid her fair share anyway, and taught her family to do the same. Her grandchildren were taught that taxes are just a larger version of the same principle. You make the strongest political case you can for what you think is right, hire a lobbyist perhaps, or write position papers or letters to the editor. But if you lose you still pay your taxes, perhaps while grumbling, but voluntarily. We who live in democracies are not naïve; we understand that part of our tax money goes for things we would not advocate. We who live in families understand the same thing: sometimes the money we earn goes to things that would not be our personal preference. Giving everyone a voice in the decision making is equally important for families and for society.

Designing a democracy is itself a fascinating subject. Economists have thought long and hard about issues like voting procedures or how to design a representational democracy. For an example that is particularly important to us, the provision of education for all children, paid for in part by people who do not have children themselves, is a part of the larger social contract that is democracy. In the education chapter coming shortly we will think about some difficult school funding questions.

An influential economist, Albert Hirschman, has argued that democracy itself requires a particular kind of good intention in the formation and articulation of political arguments: "both the public at large and its representatives—should maintain a degree of openness or tentativeness in their opinions and be ready to modify them both as a result of the arguments that will be put forward by the contending parities and, more simply, in the light of new information that will be developed in the course of public debates" (Hirschman 1989, 77). Hirschman goes on to identify and criticize the typical rhetorical stance of both conservatives and liberals. Conservatives argue that any given reform will not solve the problem, make it worse, or endanger some other more important goal. Liberals on the other hand seem to be oblivious to unintended consequences and confident in their ability to remold the world in desirable ways. As Cass Sunstein said in *The New York Review of Books* (May 23, 2013), Hirschman's intent was "to challenge intransigence on the part of both the right and the left—and to get people to listen to one another in a spirit of humility, rather than making their standard, mind-numbing rhetorical moves."

The major topics of this section—investment, education, labor conditions, and the social safety net—all require the best operation of our collective decision making. Democracy needs to work. We need to bring the wisdom and the value of good intentions we learn from our families to the political arena. We need a lot of macroeconomic thinking as well, so let's get started.

Chapter Nine

Investing in Strangers

The first thought that comes into many people's mind about "investment" is putting money in the bank or buying stocks and bonds in the financial markets. We've been talking about investment in terms of things like getting an education or starting and growing a business. These ideas of investment as "money" and investment as "doing things" are not contradictory; in fact, they are often two sides of the same coin. That might take a bit of explaining so we'll start with someone thinking of starting a business.

A business has to find a product or service that it can sell at a price that allows it to repay its costs, including servicing any debt, and still have something left over for the owners. It is not easy to find customers—at least those that will pay a reasonable amount for whatever your product is. It is not easy to find reliable people to work with, whether as partners or suppliers or employees. There are a myriad of other practical issues to deal with as well. Someone else might start a similar business nearby, the snowiest winter on record could make your ice cream less popular, or a competitor might make a real improvement in his product.

Some families or networks might be able to start a business without the help of strangers, but many times more help is needed. A shrimp fisherman who needs a boat requires the investments of many households unless he already is a rich shrimp fisherman. The people looking to start the business, shrimp fishing or ice cream making, need to find a way to borrow money, usually from people they don't know.

Anytime one household is borrowing money, another household is saving and lending. So let's think about the other side of the borrowing and lending bargain. As anybody with a brother-in-law or enterprising neighbor can tell you, it is not difficult to find someone willing to borrow your money and start a business. But it is a completely different proposition to find a borrower who will pay it back, with interest. Bankers do that for us; we put our savings into banks or other institutions of the financial markets and let the pros find the people and businesses that can make best use of our money. That might be your brother-in-law, but it might not.

Financial markets should serve the needs of both lenders and borrowers. Education aside, most investment in society goes through the financial markets, and most investment in the financial markets is in strangers. Even investments in higher education are increasingly funded by borrowing. Virtually all prosperous Americans both save and borrow, perhaps even at the same time. You may work for a business that sells bonds or equity and uses the proceeds to supply its workers with new technology or an updated facility; your retirement fund probably holds the stocks and bonds of other firms.

In chapter 16 we will acknowledge that not all money that goes into the financial markets is productively invested, but ideally it would be. In fact, ideally the money would go to those businesses or individuals that are *most* productive. Every household has to decide how much of their investment money goes to family members and how much goes into the financial markets, i.e. to strangers. We invest *for* ourselves and the people we love; we often invest *in* people we've never seen or heard of, those working for the business issuing the stocks or bonds we buy, or the business borrowing from the bank where we deposit our savings.

Saying the same thing the other way, those who love us invest a lot in us. We want to honor their investment by doing well in life. But a whole lot of perfect strangers invest in us as well. The function of the financial markets is to facilitate the latter investments.

Given that investment via the financial markets is in strangers, we also want to think about how much of that investment reaches the poor. Unfortunately, participation in the financial markets varies considerably by household income and circumstances—in a way that does not facilitate investment in or by the less prosperous. Halah Touryalai reported in *Forbes* (September 17, 2012) that in 2011, 22.5 percent of all households experiencing unemployment didn't have a checking or savings account, or anything similar. For households with incomes under $15,000 it was 28.2 percent. People who don't have a checking or savings account are unlikely to be investing, and they are also unlikely to be the recipients of loans from the ordinary financial markets.

There's an old joke that the bank will only lend you money if you don't need it. That may be an overstatement, but it is true that less prosperous households have difficulty borrowing money. Even in this day and age there may still be de facto redlining in both the housing market and in business loans. The poor have fewer assets to use as collateral. A young person from a less prosperous family may not have a cosigner. Often the only asset young people have is their own "human capital"—the economist's (perhaps clunky) way of saying their skills and abilities—and ultimately their future earning power. His or her future employment prospects may be genuinely less good than those of someone from a more prosperous background.

A story close to our hearts is about Terese, the niece of a woman whose office is on our hallway. Damage to her knees has made it impossible for her to continue at her long-time job as a stock room clerk. However, our office-mate swears she is a world-class quilter, with a terrific intuition about fabric and color juxtaposition and a one-in-a-million talent for incorporating unexpected materials into her quilts, like bits of soda bottles or shredded sponges. She has often thought about getting a webpage and selling quilts. To generate income even fabulous art quilts require finding a buyer. Her daughter could design and maintain the webpage, and Terese would love the piecing and sewing. It's the cost that stops her; the cheapest hosting site is $10 a month, with $45 to start. An industrial sewing machine and the materials for commercially viable quilts are not cheap. The quilting business could be started with an investment of $10,000—but her family has not been able to borrow that much at any interest rate. To start even such a modest business would mean less food on the table.

Microlending institutions involving far smaller amounts of money have been successfully introduced in many countries to help the poorest of the poor transition to self-employment. We will talk about them more in chapter 19, but their effectiveness in the United States has been limited. Starting a business in the United States requires navigating complex governmental regulations, and generally there is limited market demand for the items most small businesses produce because of the amount of competition from larger businesses benefiting from economies of scale. Generally U.S. microfinance lenders have not been financially self-sufficient (Talen, Weiss, and Sarkar 2002).

Much more common are the small high-interest "payday" loans available to low-income households. In "Payday Lending in America: Who Borrows, Where They Borrow, and Why," a 2012 report of the Pew Charitable Trusts, it was found that over 5 percent of adults have taken out such a loan and most typically the loans were to meet everyday expenses rather than for emergencies.[1] This kind of borrowing has been shown to exacerbate rather than alleviate economic hardship, the interest charges digging the debt hole deeper and deeper. This leads to increased difficulty paying other bills such as utilities or rent, so it is highly unlikely to lead to increased investment (Melzer 2011).

Although we touched on luck in chapter 6, we haven't talked yet about risk and uncertainty in financial investments. They are substantial and unavoidable. Even with crop insurance weather affects farmers. New competitors enter a market, or the government changes regulations or taxes. A recession might reduce customers' ability to pay. The standard way of dealing with investment risk is diversification—which for many of us means buying mutual funds. Buying a little bit of a lot of different assets is much less risky than having all your eggs in one basket, but again it is a strategy that is less available to the poor than to the middle or upper income classes. Briefly, if you can only afford one investment and the payoff seems too uncertain you don't do it—even though you might have taken the risk if you had the resources to make it a part of a larger investment package.

To summarize the chapter briefly, very large amounts of investment in our economy go through the financial markets, and that investment is in strangers. That's a great thing. Large vibrant financial markets are required for prosperity; they turn household savings into business creation and expansion. But to invest in those who have been unable to invest sufficiently in themselves, we will have to form a separate intention to do so. People who are not able to make significant investments in themselves are almost always poor, and investment via the financial markets almost never reaches the poor.

There is one important kind of investment that does not necessarily involve financial markets—education. We turn our attention now to a family's most important investment.

NOTE

1. In 2010 the average loan size was $375 and the average amount of interest paid per year was $520. The average length of loan was eighteen days, the average number of loans per year was eight.

Chapter Ten

The Wisdom of Families—The Most Important Investment

In the past families had five or eight, sometimes a dozen children. From one angle you can look at that as a diversification strategy. The more children you have the more likely at least one will survive into adulthood and be financially able to support you in your old age. But this aspect of families has drastically changed. Now as medical care improves and prosperity increases, families typically have fewer children. But we're going to argue we still diversify our investment in our children—just in a different way. We have discovered ways to diversify our education investments in each individual child.

Some children are born with a strong instinct of what they want to do with their lives. They're born mathematicians or truck drivers and even a few are born point guards. Some parents get every experience they can for their child in that one area; we know someone whose child goes to math camp, takes math courses online, reads math books in his spare time. That parent is investing in his child, but it's an all your eggs in one basket type of investment.

On the other hand, most children, people of all ages really although here we're talking about children, have many interests and abilities, and frankly there are a lot of things that seem fun at the beginning that lose their appeal over time. Getting your children into a situation where they have a real chance to experience something long enough to see how they like it requires a considerable investment of time and sometimes money. If you make it possible for a child to take the lead in a local theater production, follow the trail of the Lewis and Clark expedition, play the oboe, play on a sports team per season, throw in some math and science, then you're devoting a large amount of resources to planning and coordinating. You'll spend a lot of time and money car pooling, texting, and getting some food pulled together. You're investing as much as the parent whose child focuses on one thing, but you are diversifying your investments. As with any important family decision you have to be wise about it, not going to extremes and being clear about your motives. But essentially diversification is a great strategy.

Just as it might make sense to buy a mutual fund that holds riskier assets than you would hold individually, it might make sense to invest in aspects of your child's education that seem rather risky—if you can afford to invest in a number of other educational opportunities as well. You might pay for pricey art lessons at the Museum of Fine Arts to see whether your child's talents lie in that direction—as long as you can afford to pay for math tutoring and SAT exam preparation as well. Most colleges recommend looking into more than one major if a child's natural talents and interests are not obvious. To give a child a realistic chance at finding out whether he is good at product design or managerial accounting requires considerable investment in both fields.

It is probably obvious that this investment strategy depends on the level of family prosperity. The more prosperous the family the more investment that can be done in a child—including graduate school when relevant. But there is an interaction between scarcity and risk that has to be mentioned. These investments in your child's activities are "lumpy," you can't buy a small slice of an SAT preparation class, a small slice of math camp, and a small slice of taking the lead in a play. The evidence from behavioral economics suggests that if you can only afford to make one investment, you will not make it if it is too risky. Thus the less prosperous family might not make the single investment they could manage, say the SAT exam preparation, if family members believe that there is at best a 50-50 chance of it leading to a job in the future. They can't afford to diversify so they don't invest at all.

We'd guess that everyone with children thinks of investing in them as their most important investment and understands the family wisdom and discipline required. The next time you're tired of driving them to soccer practice or piano lessons just remind yourself you're diversifying those most important investments. In the next chapter we turn our attention to investing in the children who do not live in your house.

Chapter Eleven

Education—It's a Social Contract

Do you ever plan to retire? Do you plan to eat when you retire? Who will grow, process, transport, and sell the food you eat, perhaps cooking and serving it as well? Clearly they will be people who are working, the generations behind you, younger than you—you're retired, NOT working. Suppose you've done everything right to prepare for your retirement, in particular saved enough by any measure. Can the generations behind you make sure you starve, without breaking or changing any laws? Sure. Inflation.

Inflation can be caused by many things—but it is guaranteed if over time you have about the same number of consumers but production is falling. Are there any examples of inflation extreme enough to turn into hyperinflation? None in the United States thankfully, but many people know what happened in Germany following WWI, in Russia as it made its transition out of socialism, or more recently in Brazil between 1980 and the mid-1990s.

Now that we've gotten your attention, our point is simply that each generation must ensure that the generations behind them are productive. The more productive they are the less the risk of hyperinflation, and the more likely you will be able to eat when you don't work—the basic idea of retirement.

When we talk about this with students who tend to be in their twenties someone invariably notices that the prosperity of each generation depends on the generations *behind* them. You have good reason to invest in your children. But wouldn't those in the working generation be better off to put all their savings into their kids, and arrange things so that people in the elderly generation starve? As we mentioned above, inflation is one way to do that. Inevitably some student, we presume tongue in cheek, proposes putting the grandmas out on the ice floe. (Not their own grandparents exactly, other people's.)

This is an awkward moment in class; we're the older generation they're talking about. Some other student eventually will rescue us—and not only on humanitarian grounds. Even if you don't "care" about anybody but yourself (our students are quite humane, but just saying), even if you don't care about the elderly per se, you will eventually "be" the retired generation. No one wants to work past the day their health gets problematic. If your children see you abandon your parents, what on earth do you think they will do to you? So in effect each working generation always agrees to support the elderly, *and* support and invest in the children. This is one of the most essential social contracts we have. The alternative is working until you die, which was quite common a few generations ago.

There is a serious sense in which each working generation is a sandwich generation regardless of whether your parents are still living or whether you have children. You will notice that the argument here is that we all must invest in children, whether or not we have any children of our own. Our future prosperity as an economy depends on the productivity of all children.

What proportion of U.S. children live in poverty? More than one in five—the poverty rate for children in 2012 was almost 22 percent. The rate was lowest among children claiming White, Non-Hispanic as their race, just over 12 percent, and highest among those identifying themselves as Black, almost 38 percent; for those identifying themselves as Hispanic the poverty rate among children was almost 34 percent.[1] We don't burden you with many statistics in this book, but this is an important one. We must take care of the generations behind us so they can be productive when we need them to be during our own retirement. Because about 20 percent of children are poor, that means caring for poor children as well. To ignore poor children would mean that there are potentially as many as 20 percent fewer productive workers in the future. (We don't mean to imply for an instant that children are valued only as workers, but whether they are productive as a generation does matter enormously for prosperity and inflation.) And probably those people would require some welfare support as well, a double whammy.

Yes, we understand that by global or historical standards the current poor are not doing all that badly. But they are comparing themselves to us, not to their ancestors or to people half a world away. And besides, being a poor child in the United States today still means cockroaches in the kitchen sink. It means that it's not safe to walk home from school alone. It means living in areas with high crime rates of all sorts and constant fear of mugging even in daylight. Pat is often at an inner-city neighborhood agency late enough that it is dark in the winter months, and even if her car is in the parking lot the staff watches to make sure she gets out safely. It means limited access to supermarkets and high prices at small local food shops. Elana can't take a job too far from the bus route, and when her daughter became a Certified Medical

Assistant it took quite a while for her to find a job she could get to without a car.

Anyone of any age in any era with a drop of humanity in them has always known that we have to invest in our children. For the purposes of this book, the question is who "our" children are. Should we educate the children of strangers exactly the same way we educate the children who live in our house or are a part of our personal network? If I am willing to make more sacrifices for my child than you are, shouldn't my child get a head start over yours? But then how do you measure sacrifice? Market thinking simplifies that question: it measures sacrifice by dollars spent. Family thinking complicates everything because it says, well, maybe sacrifice should be measured as the fraction of income available that is spent on the children, or something else altogether.

Once we confront school spending formulas from anything other than a strict market point of view it becomes necessary to think about equality and fairness. There is nothing we have stronger feelings about than that our children should be treated fairly. We have found the insights of Amartya Sen, whom we introduced in chapter 4, to be quite helpful. Briefly, the relevant insight here is that you can only equalize in one way. And once you have chosen what will be equalized, in every other way people will be treated unequally.[2] Suppose you decide, for a simple example, that it is fair for everyone to pay a given proportion of their income, say 5 percent, to educate their children. Just the mere fact that some families have one child and others have two or five would mean that different amounts would be spent per child. Setting that difficulty aside, 5 percent of $35,000 is a whole lot less money than 5 percent of $100,000, so the child of the more prosperous family gets a huge head start over the child of the middle income family. On the other hand, you can spend the same dollar amount per child, but that will require that people on the upper end of the income distribution pay not only for their own children but some of the cost of the children of people whose income is below the median as well.

Market economies don't worry about these issues. Each family spends what it chooses given its resources on education as on everything else. People who reject that answer because it's unfair have to grapple with quite difficult issues; real families and family networks talk almost endlessly about them. The design of the education system can and should be done as intelligently as possible to negotiate between these points of view, to do justice both to the sacrifices some parents make as well as to the children of those unwilling or unable to make sacrifices for them. In our home state of Illinois, for example, the state grant to a local school district is a fixed amount per child. But the local funding is a percent of the local property tax assessment and, therefore, related to the taxpayers' wealth. In addition, individual school organizations do fund-raisers and there are sometimes special fees to participate in programs such as music groups or sports teams.

In the United States the evidence is that our education funding systems do not necessarily favor the poor. James Poterba (1997) examines the effect of demographics on K-12 education spending and finds that "over the 1960-1990 period . . . an increase in the fraction of elderly residents in a jurisdiction is associated with a significant reduction in per-child educational spending. This reduction is particularly large when the elderly residents and the school-age population are from different racial groups" (Poterba 1997, 48).[3]

We don't want to imply that decent education is just a matter of getting the funding formulas about right.[4] Education is a difficult subject with lots of research left to be done about what helps children achieve better outcomes and what doesn't, but we have learned some things. Levitt and Dubner (2005, 166–68) examine the factors that contribute to children's educational success (defined as high test scores). Having highly educated parents with a high socioeconomic status tops the list of factors positively and strongly correlated with educational success. Other positive factors are a mother thirty or older at the birth of her first child, speaking English in the home, having many books in the home, being adopted, and having parents involved in PTA. In chapter 6 we touched briefly on how luck affects educational outcomes, especially a lottery system for admittance into desirable schools. In Levitt and Dubner's data, winning such lotteries has no particular effect on educational outcomes. However, those students whose parents cared enough about education to enter the lottery, whether or not they won, were more likely to graduate from high school than those whose parents did not enter them (Levitt and Dubner 2005, 158–59).

Levitt and Dubner's list of things that are not correlated with educational success has a few surprises. The data suggest that at least on average such things as moving to a better neighborhood, parents reading to children, attending Head Start, going to museums, encouraging children to not watch much television, and having a mother that doesn't work between birth and kindergarten are not correlated with educational success. What makes this evidence so compelling is that it is based on a large comprehensive data set collected by the U.S. Department of Education in the 1990s, and the statistical techniques are first rate.

Levitt and Dubner's explanation is that the most important determinants of a child's educational success are the parents, but "most of the things that matter were decided long ago [before the child was born]—who you are, whom you married, what kind of life you lead. If you are smart, hardworking, well educated, well paid, and married to someone equally fortunate, then your children are more likely to succeed. . . . But it isn't so much a matter of what you *do* as a parent; it's who you are" (italics in the original) (2005,

175). And what they mean by "who you are" is mainly how educated you are and what your income is. As we suggested in the last chapter, we'd like to believe what you do matters too, but no one is denying that children with prosperous parents get a head start education-wise.

Although the basic relationship between education, income, and unemployment is probably common knowledge, still the size of the effects can be surprising. In 2012 the median weekly income for full time workers age 25 and older with a high school education was $652. While some college and an associate's degree each increased weekly income, it was by such a modest amount that income for these groups still did not reach the median for all groups of $815. Median income for someone with a bachelor's degree was $1,066, the first one over the median for all groups. Not surprisingly, further increases in education continued to increase income as well.[5]

Unemployment rates have a similar pattern, but this time we must mention that the situation for those without a high school diploma is quite difficult, with an unemployment rate of 12.4 percent in 2012. A high school diploma cut the rate by a third to 8.3 percent; a bachelor's degree cut that almost in half to 4.5 percent, and having a professional degree halved it again to 2.1 percent. Luttmer has compared the recovery in employment following the 2008 crisis by educational levels with some cautionary results for the less educated. Those without a high school diploma "suffered a 10 percent job decline" by 2013 (Clement 2013, 41). But employment for college graduates was up compared to 2008 by well over 5 percent—in normal times nothing to be proud of but at least positive. The difference has everything to do with innovation in the economy: "One employee type—managers—has a skill with higher value given current product prices. A recession presents an opportunity for new project creation, so managerial skills are treasured. Since less-educated employees tend to be workers rather than managers, they are likely to suffer more job losses when a recession lowers spending on the consumption goods they produce" (Clement 2013, 41).

Clearly, prosperity is associated with good educational outcomes. It seems natural to wonder then whether simply increasing the income of families where the children struggle with educational goals would help. Economists have studied this question quite carefully over many years, and the answer is not nearly as clear cut as we would like. Many a study has found no relationship between family income and a child's educational attainment.[6] The difficulty is to separate out the effects of other household characteristics, such as parental involvement or education, from the effects of income per se. In real life these variables are interconnected, but to study the effect of just one—income—requires being able to isolate it.

There is one study, however, what economists call a "natural experiment," which avoids this statistical problem. Briefly, because of the way the revenue from a new casino on the Eastern Cherokee reservation in North

Carolina was distributed, researchers could separate the effects of income from parental characteristics. What they found was that the increased income did increase the likelihood of the children graduating from high school by age nineteen. Interestingly, the results were largely driven by the poorest households. "An additional $4,000 per year for the poorest households increases educational attainment by one year at age 21, and reduces the chances of committing a minor crime by 22 percent for 16 and 17 year olds" (Akee et al. 2010, 86). Just as interesting are the empirical results concerning which parent received the increase in income: "mothers who receive the exogenous increase in incomes affect the child's educational outcome, while fathers who receive the income affect the child's criminal behavior" (Akee et al. 2010, 90).

This evidence is somewhat more encouraging about society's ability to improve the educational outcomes of the less advantaged members of the economy than Levitt and Dubner's evidence. But it's only one study and with an avowedly small (1,420 children) and non-diverse sample. The note of caution this introduces has led economists to consider other ways to try to improve educational outcomes. Economists believe in incentives. Unfortunately, incentive systems have not been successful in education. Economist Roland Fryer has done a lot of work on the effectiveness of incentives in public school like "offering bonuses to teachers if they improved their classes' test results; offering incentives like cell-phone minutes to students if they improved their own test results; offering families financial incentives if their children did better" (Tough 2012, 66). Although there were a few exceptions, "for the most part, the programs were a bust. The biggest experiment, which offered incentives to teachers in New York City, cost seventy-five million dollars and took three years to conduct. And in the spring of 2011, Fryer reported that it had produced no positive results at all" (Tough 2012, 66). At a minimum these results suggests that designing a functional incentive system is no walk in the park. Levitt and some other coauthors have done some preliminary small scale studies which suggest that one behavioral economic insight discussed in the previous section might be useful here. In a field experiment setting, students respond more strongly to incentives framed as losses compared to gains, financial incentives mean more to older children and less to younger children, and the incentives need to be essentially immediate (Levitt et al. 2012). But behavioral economics is no silver bullet and some behavioral economists are highly skeptical about incentives in education (Ariely 2008, 85).

There is also some evidence that design of the education system should reflect differing incomes. For example, consider the question of whether or not it's better for learning to have a long summer vacation. For reading skills, poor children are disadvantaged: "Poor kids may out-learn rich kids during the school year. But during the summer, they fall far behind" (Gladwell

2008, 258). In fact, "virtually all of the advantage that wealthy students have over poor students is the result of differences in the way privileged kids learn while they are *not* in school" (italics in the original) (Gladwell 2008, 258). The implication is that our long summer vacations help middle and upper income children; they do not help lower income children. It may be time to consider the idea of different lengths of the school year for students with different levels of prosperity. Some school districts now offer special programs during the summer at schools in low income areas.

It occurs to us that class size might be a similar issue. There is nearly universal agreement that a lot of kids stuck in a small classroom with one overworked teacher is not good for learning. In the United States almost half of the states have passed legislation to encourage (or force in some instances) reduction in class size in grades K-12. Malcolm Gladwell suggests that class sizes in the upper teens or the twenties are best under normal circumstances in the context of an argument that classes can be too small as well as too large (Gladwell 2013, 53ff). We notice, however, that his anecdotal evidence of classes being too small is for schools serving the very prosperous, which leads us to wonder whether that's ever a problem for schools at the other end of the income continuum.[7]

There is another thorny issue that has to be addressed. Is education an "investment" in the sense of increasing future income-earning ability because of the content of what is learned, the reading, writing, and arithmetic, so to speak? Or is the investment aspect of education something entirely different? Is it the fact that one learns discipline by studying almost any academic subject? For example, how effective is studying for the GED (General Educational Development) exam in preparing students for adult life as compared to regular high school graduation? If a GED is as good as high school, then the answer would be that it is the content that matters, the 3-Rs. But if a GED is not as good as high school, then the implication is that what students get from school is much more than the material covered.

The answer is the latter. In general, GED holders and high school graduates score about the same on various achievement tests, but other results are very different. Paul Tough (2012, xviii) summarizes a study by James Heckman, one of the most influential economists currently thinking about education, as follows:

> GED recipients weren't *anything* like high-school graduates. At age twenty-two, Heckman found, just 3 percent of GED recipients were enrolled in a four-year university or had completed some kind of post-secondary degree, compared to 46 percent of high-school graduates. In fact, . . . when you consider all kinds of important future outcomes—annual income, unemployment rate, divorce rate, use of illegal drugs—GED recipients look exactly like high-school dropouts, despite the fact that they have earned this supposedly valuable extra

> credential, and despite the fact that they are, on average, considerably more intelligent than high-school dropouts." (italics in the original)

It appears that GED recipients typically lack some psychological skills that high school graduates have acquired. School per se seems valuable.

As is often the case, problems that are hard enough for the middle and upper classes are even more intractable for the poor. Successfully negotiating the educational system—temporarily making the heroic assumption that it is well designed—is much more difficult when children are economically disadvantaged. Paul Tough argues that the tacit knowledge that middle and upper income kids have been immersed in their whole lives is like a foreign language to lower income kids. One of his primary ideas is that character matters, but that poor children need more of it than income-advantaged students do. Character

> can function as a substitute for the social safety net that students at Riverdale [one of New York's most prestigious private schools] enjoy—the support from their families and schools and culture that protects them from the consequences of occasional detours and mistakes and bad decisions. If you don't have that kind of safety net—and children in low-income families almost by definition do not—you need to compensate in another way. To succeed, you need more grit, more social intelligence, more self-control than wealthier kids. Developing that strength takes a lot of work. (Tough 2012, 103)

He goes on to argue that a disadvantaged person who does graduate from college will have "climbed a mountain" to get there, and may actually have some real advantages over more privileged kids in terms of character building. Our friend Sandy particularly admires Supreme Court Justice Sonia Sotomayor. Although she was disadvantaged by her economic background, she gained character by having to try harder.

Paul Tough is reasonably optimistic about our being able to help students succeed. His view is that a child's success depends as much on non-cognitive skills as on cognitive ones, and that these non-cognitive skills like "grit, curiosity, self-control, and optimism" can be taught (Tough 2012, 122, 196 and elsewhere). The suggestion is that while it can be taught by teachers in a traditional school setting, it needn't be taught that way. Mentors and role models can be great teachers as well.[8] Elana's grandson has a mentor from his church who is also his scout master. He encourages the boy to do well in school, rewarding him with special treats and gifts for good work. One advantage of a mentor is that the child then has someone special to care about, to try to please perhaps. Working parents, especially those income-patching with two or more part-time jobs, may not always have the time or emotional energy to offer the extra bit of encouragement that makes a real difference.

Our friend Elana is especially concerned about children living in poverty who drop out of school altogether. For girls the cause is often early pregnancy. According to the Centers for Disease Prevention, by age twenty-two about 90 percent of women who have not had a child have graduated from high school. The equivalent fraction for teen mothers is 50 percent. For boys, unfortunately, the cause is often that they believe they can do better selling drugs than getting a conventional job.

Levitt and Dubner recount the situation in Chicago in the 1990s and 2000s. "To the kids growing up in a housing project on Chicago's south side, crack dealing was a glamour profession. For many of them, the job of gang boss—highly visible and highly lucrative—was easily the best job they thought they had access to" (Levitt and Dubner 2005, 105). Further,

> the gang also presented an opportunity for longtime employment. Before crack, it was just about impossible to earn a living in a street gang. . . . But with crack, there was real money to be made. . . . This was happening just as the old-fashioned sort of life-time jobs—factory jobs especially—were disappearing. In the past, a semi-skilled black man in Chicago could earn a decent wage working in a factory. With that option narrowing, crack dealing looked even better. (Levitt and Dubner 2005, 112)

But only for a few at the top; most drug sellers still made very low wages, well below the minimum wage, not to mention being in and out of prison and having a high probability of being a victim of violence (Levitt and Dubner 2005, 103). Echoing Levitt's results, Elana sees that as early as fifth or sixth grade many boys in low income families lose their drive to do well in school because of the number of idle men they see in their neighborhoods. She also believes that seeing highly paid professional athletes on TV results in their playing sports and ignoring their homework after school.

Education is important to all of us. We understand there are problems, and we hunger for answers, strategies, policies. The economic evidence certainly suggests that a "one size fits all" policy prescription is never going to work. We ourselves believe in mentoring. Frankly we find it quite depressing that the economic evidence of a positive effect of mentoring on future employment does not yet exist. Partly the response has to be better science, more experiments, better experimental design. The technological revolution in data collection, management, and analysis changes the landscape in ways that would have been unimaginable an intellectual generation ago. But partly the response has to be pragmatic. Try things. See if they work. At the end of the day nothing is more important to an economy than education. The path forward is through good intentions, good science focusing on the insights of behavioral economics, and our collective moral imagination.

NOTES

1. U.S. Census Bureau, Current Population Survey, 2013 Annual Social and Economic Supplement, POV01.

2. To be technical, for two highly correlated dimensions to equalize along one means to almost equalize along the other. But in real life a high correlation between all important aspects of a given problem is the exception not the rule.

3. It goes without saying that issues of race and class are ubiquitous in education as a whole—and that many of these issues have direct financial implications. Leonard Pitts in the Peoria *Journal Star* (November 28, 2012) for example, argues that racial differences in reading goals related to the No Child Left Behind Act's subsidy schemes should have an expiration date. Lynn Freehill, editor of the University of Texas alumni magazine (July/August 2012), argues in favor of class-based admissions at the University of Texas even with all the vexing implications for the University finances.

4. Although Jannett does have some ideas on whether the federal or state government should use a cost sharing or reward for performance approach to helping local districts improve performance. For this discussion in another context please see, Gretz, Highfill, and Scott (2012).

5. U.S. Bureau of Labor Statistics, Current Population Survey, Employment Projections, Earnings and Unemployment Rates by Educational Attainment. To be absolutely accurate, persons with professional degrees have a higher median income than those with doctoral degrees. The unemployment data which follows is from the same source.

6. See the literature review in Akee et al. (2010, 87).

7. We also have to acknowledge that expenditures on reducing class size should be compared against other possible uses for the funds, and that the effect of increasing class sizes on education outcomes depends crucially on how any teacher lay-offs are done, for example whether based on seniority or teacher effectiveness (Chingos 2013).

8. In February 2014 President Obama launched the "My Brother's Keeper Initiative to Build Ladders of Opportunity For Boys and Young Men of Color." The initial response to the initiative has been positive from at least some commentators from both ends of the political spectrum.

Chapter Twelve

Mother Jones Would Be Pretty Happy

On Interstate 55 near the exit for Mount Carmel, Illinois, a sign reads *Mother Jones Monument*. It marks the burial place of Mary Harris Jones, who looked like a gentle grandmother but in fact was a fiery-tongued union organizer in the confrontational days of the Robber Barons. In a 2001 biography Elliott Gorn writes: "In place of the untrammeled rule of the marketplace, she substituted her metaphor of the family of labor, which assumed that all change must be directed toward creating humane communities."[1] Although the juxtaposition of marketplace and humane communities resonates with the theme of this book, the labor markets of Mother Jones's time were very different from those facing workers in the United States today. Violence was common as strikers battled strikebreakers and one union battled another, with state militia and occasionally federal troops brought in to the quell the riots.

For many of us turning our educational investments into income requires time spent in the labor market. Most of us will earn essentially all of our pre-retirement income working for others. Even many people who plan to start a business gain experience and rent money by working for other businesses. The labor market is so important we've already touched on several aspects of it, noting some relevant insights from behavioral economics, and we ended section I with some implications for persons without flexibility to look for new jobs. Sections VI looks toward the future of work.

For this chapter we begin our thinking with some basics of the labor market, remembering what it was like in the distant past as compared to more recent times. Although this is a simple example, imagine someone looking for a job who has decided the least he will work for is $20 an hour. Such decisions are complex, but taking everything into account, that's what he requires before he'll take a job. Imagine someone else is looking to hire, and it's a job that person would qualify for. The potential employer's decision is also complex, but suppose he's figured out that the most he is willing to pay someone is $30 an hour. This is promising; there's a deal to be made here. If they live in a "small-town" world of a moderate number of businesses and potential workers, especially if everyone knows everyone else, what wage they actually agree on is probably determined by many factors: how good a negotiator each person is, whether they are members of a larger family network or social organization, what is considered customary in a given place and time.

Probably in the distant past, that's how wages were determined. But as the world became more industrialized, starting about 1850 to pick a somewhat arbitrary date, things began to change. Our students at the University sometimes talk about a "buyer's market" or a "seller's market" for a particular major in a given year. What they essentially mean is in that year there are more people looking for jobs than firms hiring, a buyer's market, or the reverse, more firms trying to hire than there are qualified candidates, a seller's market. As economies became more market dominated, wages were increasingly determined by such factors. In our simple example, whether the actual wage is closer to $20 or $30 depends on the relative number of buyers and sellers. In the early industrial period, approximately the second half of the nineteenth century and the first half of the twentieth, it was increasingly the case that wages were determined in buyer's markets.

Although the actual labor markets were more complicated than this, you might think of a small town with one major employer, a mill or a factory or a mine, and many men trying to get work there. In that extreme case of a buyer's market, the wages will be $20 for everyone. The employer was willing to pay $30, but wouldn't have to, thus his profits are $10 more an hour than he would have been willing to live with. Let's think about why this is. Suppose there is one worker who understands that the employer was willing to pay more than $20 and holds out for $25. The man standing beside him, who also wants to get hired, says to himself if I say I'll work for $24, then I'll get the job and my neighbor holding out for $25 will be out of luck. The first guy, realizing that $23 is better than no job at all, undercuts the second guy's wage offer—the process continuing until both (and all) workers are getting paid the minimum they are willing to work for.

In the early days of industrialization economists would refer to something called "the iron law of wages." They meant that each worker's reservation wage, the lowest wage they were willing to work for, was the amount required to not starve. The workers who got hired at that wage survived, barely. Those not hired, starved. The labor market in the early days of industrialization was tough.

What the early labor leaders like Mother Jones realized was that the reason wages were driven down to starvation rates was because one worker was bidding against another for a job. If the workers could be persuaded to forgo bidding against each other, the wage each worker received would be higher. To say the same thing in modern terms, forming a union turned a buyer's market into a situation that was neither a buyer's market nor a seller's market. In the simple case of one union and one employer, the wages would be negotiated between them. The workers could reasonably bargain for $25, perhaps $26 or $27, in our example. The original tactic of the labor organizers was a strike, with considerable social unrest and violence resulting. Social, religious, and political pressures eventually resulted in federal legislation being passed in the 1930s. In 1935 the National Labor Relations Act provided for unions to organize a plant or company by election rather than through a strike. Labor and labor rights would be a part of the economic landscape from then on.

In 1938 the Fair Labor Standards Act established a federal minimum wage and set the forty-hour work week, with overtime pay beyond that. The original minimum wage was set at 25 cents per hour and covered about 43 percent of wage earners. But the essential argument in its favor is again that it prohibits workers from bidding against each other to bring wages down to starvation levels, and it does so regardless of the number of potential workers or employers. Since 1938 both the hourly rate and coverage have steadily increased, and many states have a higher minimum wage than the federal one. About 90 percent of workers are now covered, and the federal rate reached $7.25 in 2009. As you are well aware, however, prices have increased faster than this since 1938, resulting in a loss of purchasing power over time.

After World War II, the pendulum swung back the other way when the Labor Management Relations Act of 1947 restricted some union activities and allowed for the decertification of a union. Union membership in the civilian labor force peaked at about one-third during WWII. Union wage and salary workers in the nation's civilian noninstitutional population age sixteen and over was 11.3 percent in 2013, down from 20.1 percent in 1983, the first year the current data series was available.[2] Although there has been increasing unionization of government workers during this period, over 35 percent in 2013, it has been more than offset by the decline in private sector unionization, which is down to less than 7 percent of the private sector workforce. Another piece of evidence suggesting the decline in the importance of unions is that nine of the ten states with the fastest job growth between 2002 and 2012 have passed "Right-to-Work" legislation according to an advocacy group.[3]

Part of the decline of unionization is attributed to public backlash at union corruption, but probably it's mostly a result of changes in technology. We will have much to say in later chapters about the effects of technology on the economy, but unionization is less common in high tech industries. It is also less common in the service industries that increasingly absorb a higher proportion of the workforce.

Two more outcomes of the labor movement deserve mention. The first occurred during the early 1940s. In responding to the wage freeze of WWII, unionized firms started offering pensions and health insurance as inducements in recruiting workers, and non-union firms had to keep up with these efforts to retain their workers. In 1970, pressure from union lobbying was instrumental in the passage of the Occupational Safety and Health Act, setting standards to limit the risk of work-related injuries and exposure to toxic substances. While there are some unintended side effects of these policies, now both union and non-union workplaces are much cleaner and safer than Mother Jones ever would have dreamed possible.

What we have learned from behavioral economics suggests that most of us are not very good at evaluating risks and weighing the importance of the present compared to the future. Therefore a (young) worker might be willing to take on a risky job for a higher wage (especially if the health effects would be felt later in life). But some other worker might bid against that worker for the job, accepting a slightly smaller wage for taking on the risk. In that case the competition between them for the job might well result in one of them ending up with the job at a wage that does not compensate him for the extra risk.[4] In that case all workers might well be grateful for federal legislation prohibiting this kind of competition between them.

While everyone has benefited from these changes, the effect of the minimum wage is probably most important to people in the lower reaches of the income distribution. The minimum wage is rarely relevant for unionized workers, but it is for young persons, persons in service industries, and the poor. Workers younger than twenty-five accounted for about half of those earning minimum wage in 2012, and about 60 percent of minimum wage workers were in service occupations, many in the fast food industry.[5]

The potential downside of both unions and the minimum wage was understood from the beginning. Hypothetically, if a potential employer has decided that the most he is willing to pay a new employee is $5 an hour, then a minimum wage of $8 an hour means that he won't hire that new worker. A person who might have been willing to work for $5 an hour won't have a job. The empirical question of whether the minimum wage reduces employment is one of the most heavily studied in economics, and the answer appears to be that, yes, it does. Recently Meer and West have suggested that the most important effect of an increasing minimum wage is to reduce "net job growth, primarily through its effect on job creation by expanding establishments" (Meer and West 2013). That is, business employment would have grown more in the absence of a minimum wage, exactly as our theory suggests. An earlier comprehensive high-quality survey found similar results (Neumark and Wascher 2006). Thus it appears that the effect of the minimum wage is to increase wages for those who have a job, but to reduce the number of jobs or hours available.

Given this tradeoff, it is perhaps not surprising that it's still a live political issue. As reported by Catherine Rampell and Steven Greenhouse in *The New York Times* (November 7, 2013) The Fair Minimum Wage Act of 2013 was introduced in both the House and Senate, proposing an increase to $10.10 an hour by 2015 and tying it to the cost of living thereafter. On the fiftieth anniversary of the March on Washington and the "I Have a Dream" speech by Dr. Martin Luther King Jr., fast food workers around the nation staged a one day strike asking for a minimum wage of $15 an hour, as reported by Pam Adams in the Peoria *Journal Star* (August 30, 2013). They garnered lots of publicity, successfully pointing up the income gap between workers and the top management of the fast food chains, although it is notable that there was none of the violence of Mother Jones's time.[6] There is beginning to be traction in the media for the idea that increasing wages for people at or barely above the minimum wage might pay off for everyone—worker, employer, and customer alike. Adam Davidson in *The New York Times Magazine* (January 5, 2014) argues that workers who feel valued are more engaged in their work, creating an environment where customers are more likely to feel their needs are being met—and thus buy more—which increases revenue sufficiently to have a positive effect on the bottom line.

No one claims that the proposed federal minimum wage of $10.10 an hour would be high enough to provide a living wage for a full time worker with a family of four. It would have to be a part of an income patching strategy as mentioned in chapter 2. But as reported by Annie Lowrey in *The New York Times* (January 5, 2014), Arindrajit Dube estimates that this increase in the minimum wage would bring a 1.7 percent reduction in the poverty rate among working-age Americans and help about five million people. Nevertheless, the problem with using the minimum wage to help the poor is the fact that many part-time minimum-wage workers are from prosperous families. These include both teenagers and retired persons with an adequate pension. Many people believe the Earned Income Tax Credit, discussed in the next chapter, is a more focused policy for helping the poor.

Lack of work is a different problem for the poor than poorly paid work, and again the age of the worker seems to play a role. Although the unemployment rate falls steadily as the age of workers increases, the duration of unemployment does just the opposite. For workers sixteen to nineteen years old the median duration of unemployment in 2012 was nine and a half weeks, meaning that half found work faster than that. But the duration of unemployment rose for older workers, the median rising to almost thirty-one weeks for workers fifty-five to sixty-four years old.[7] A number of factors may be involved. Some older workers can afford to be more choosey about which job offer to accept. Employers may be less willing to take on a worker closer to retirement because of potential medical costs or because the investment in worker training has to pay off over a shorter period of time.

We've covered the main features of the labor movement, but we want to remember that working hard and smart is absolutely key to a prosperous economy. We sometimes use the word "labor" to mean only those working for a wage, but economists often use the term for anyone working outside the home for money, from the CEO of a Fortune 50 company to your babysitter. Virtually everyone is involved in the labor market in the larger sense for broad stretches of their lives. The labor market gives us an idea of what we can most productively contribute to the economy. To oversimplify a bit, before a business decides to hire someone they must do a lot of homework—figure out what good or service that person will help produce, what customers would be willing to pay for it, how that position will contribute to the overall process of providing that service or good to customers. The pay they offer for the position will reflect that thinking.

The economists' shorthand is that wages are signals. If one job you're thinking of pays a lot more than another, then that's a signal to you that others "value" that activity more—value in the sense of strangers being willing to put their money on the line to reward it. There's nothing that says you have to take the higher paying job; there are many other aspects about a job that can affect that decision.

Prosperity is driven by accurate signals from the labor market, but it's by no means a perfect system. Changes in economic and social policy may be required to deal with the problem of too few jobs or age discrimination. Social Security, unemployment insurance, and the Earned Income Tax Credit are all a part of the social safety net which is the subject of the next chapter.

For the moment, we'll conclude with a return to Mother Jones's idea that labor needed to form a kind of social contract of its own, to act as a family in a way. You and your family can be glad that the labor movement has progressed to where most jobs are safer now, the threat of violence is reduced, and more people earn a living wage. While there is still room for improvement, Mother Jones probably would be more than just happy; she might be thrilled.

NOTES

1. See, Elliott J. Gorn (2001), *Mother Jones: The Most Dangerous Woman in America*; the quotation is from page 302.
2. U.S. Bureau of Labor Statistics, Union Members Summary, January 24. 2014.
3. See analysis of 2012 BEA data in the *National Right to Work Newsletter* (October 2013) "Right to Work States: Superior Job Growth."
4. For details on how this might work itself out see Frank (1985, 140 ff).
5. U.S. Bureau of Labor Statistics, Current Population Survey, Characteristics of Minimum Wage Workers: 2012. Age is table 1; occupations is table 4.

6. At the other end of the income spectrum, Ron Unz, a "Silicon Valley multimillionaire and registered Republican who once ran for governor and, briefly, U.S. Senate" has suggested raising the minimum wage in California to $12 an hour (Peoria *Journal Star*, January 12, 2014).

7. U.S. Bureau of Labor Statistics, Current Population Survey, Characteristics of the Unemployed: 2012. Table 31.

Chapter Thirteen

The Best Nets Are More Holes Than Rope

Poverty in the 1960s and 1970s in the United States could be described by a single word: elderly. Thankfully, that is no longer true, largely because of Social Security and Medicare (Taylor 2012, 93). As with financial markets these programs can't be understood without thinking in macro terms. We've heard people refer to Social Security as a Ponzi scheme—and it is true that the taxes paid in by current workers don't go to an "investment fund"—they go to current retirees.[1] But of course, in chapter 11 we reminded ourselves the elderly always have to rely on the people younger than they are for current production. At the basic level of humanity, whatever economic institutions we have, the old must always rely on the young.

It seems to be a highly contentious political issue whether the financial market or Social Security is the better way to finance retirement; we would argue for a healthy dose of both. On the one hand financial markets may be more efficient in some ways—certainly efficiency is supposed to be one of the benefits of markets. On the other hand, risk is ubiquitous; if the way to deal with it is diversification, then there is no wider pool to diversify over than the entire economy, that is, let the federal government take the investment risk.[2] Thus we would argue it makes sense to have a socially determined minimum retirement payment, called Social Security, that is guaranteed by the government. Working people who want more than this minimum could save and invest in the financial market—that is, we advocate roughly the system we have now. However, we would make Social Security payments fully taxable income, partly shifting the focus of Social Security toward being a safety net for the poor rather than an entitlement for persons of all income.

Whether you agree with our specific ideas or not, the larger point is that Social Security and Medicare are as much a part of the intergenerational social contract as the government provided education we talked about in chapter 11. We educate our children partly to support us when we get old. Social Security and Medicare are the primary programs by which the younger generations support the older generations. We always remind our students that before Social Security became common grandparents and grandchildren generally shared the same living quarters even for the middle and upper income classes. You shared your bathroom with your grandfather.[3]

Imagine a young adult who graduates from college on Saturday and has a great job lined up that starts Monday morning at nine o'clock. On Sunday she goes sky diving to celebrate. Her parachute malfunctions and she sustains injuries that require multiple interventions and years of rehab. For whatever set of reasons good or bad, that one Sunday she was not covered by health insurance. Although we have changed the details a bit, heartbreakingly this is a true story; it happened to one of our students. The question is who pays for her care? Her family or society at large? If society decides that her family should pay, and they cannot afford the appropriate healthcare, then the woman is never able to get back on her feet enough health-wise to make anything like the contribution to society she was set up to make as a college graduate. Make no mistake; usually families without health insurance cannot afford to pay for this scale of healthcare. Efficiency then would imply society should pay so that the woman will become a contributing member of the economy for years to come. Except, of course, for the moral hazard. Everyone knows jumping out of airplanes is risky; you have to sign a release to that effect. It makes sense for the government to provide medical services that more than pay for themselves in terms of the future productivity of the people being helped, except that some people might be tempted to abuse the system. Frankly, we don't know what to do about the moral hazard here; we hope everyone is thinking hard about the problem. Some of our thoughts can be found in chapter 23.

Unemployment insurance and disability insurance are also a part of the social safety net. Daron Acemoglu argues that these are highly related, especially in the current economy. He notes the effect of changing technology on the work environment.

> [The] types of bread-and-butter jobs of previous decades have gone; now those tasks are being performed by robots and computers, and instead we have an explosion of demand in the service sector, in middle- and low-skill services, for example, in health care, clerical occupations or customer service. These are jobs that workers with high school or two-year college degrees can perform. But for the most part, U.S. workers, especially U.S. males, haven't really made the transition to performing them. (Clement 2011, 20)

Our economy is producing jobs, just not the relatively well paid manufacturing jobs that many men (a few women, but mostly men) relied on for decades. One of the surprising consequences is for disability programs. "A lot of people who get discouraged because the sort of jobs they were expecting don't exist, drop out of the labor market. So, disability rolls, for example, have exploded, mostly with low-skilled males who are frustrated because they're not finding the sort of jobs they hoped for" (Clement 2011, 20). He goes on to say that these workers aren't faking disability, but the standards have become more accommodating especially in places where low-skilled workers have a particularly hard time finding employment.

The essential problem is program design. Technological change is generally a great thing. In the long run in terms of economic growth, it's much better to have a robot doing repetitive dangerous tasks than a human being, freeing up the human being to do those things that only humans can do. But for the actual live human beings who had those jobs—that's hard news to hear, especially if the jobs were relatively well paying and the workers are middle aged. Retraining is more difficult for a fifty-five year old than for a twenty-five year old. The social safety net must balance family and market concerns. It would be fatal to an economy to forbid technological progress, but it's a case of the benefits of better products, safer workplaces, and so on, going to the many and the losses going to the few—the actual workers laid off.[4] This is an issue we will revisit in chapter 22.

When most poor were elderly, the social safety net solution was relatively straightforward (i.e., Social Security and Medicare). To be blunt, elderly people need to eat; usually they do not need to be moved into the workforce. They do not have infant children needing education. But "for some years now the group that is disproportionately poor has been best described as single-parent households headed by a woman" (Taylor 2012, 93–94). Poverty now is a much harder problem than it was in the 1970s.

We mentioned the parable often found in economics textbooks about teaching a man to fish. There's a lot of truth in that, but he won't be able to learn if he's starving. In the modern world you give him some money, whatever you think is the minimum for him to get by, and then you expect him to live on that and learn to fish. To be concrete, suppose you give him a welfare payment of $2000 a month to support his family. Income-earning opportunities in our economy are not all or nothing. It's not the case that you make either $2000 minimum or you make nothing. Now suppose he manages to find some work, and makes $500 in a given month. (Make it December; he's doing seasonal labor.) The question is do you now give him only $1500 on the reasoning that $1500 + $500 is what he needs? If you adopt that strategy you're creating an implicit tax rate of 100 percent. For each dollar he earns he loses a dollar of welfare; working makes him exactly no better off than when he was not working. Even a cursory understanding of incentives suggests that is crazy. Why would he work, or try to better his job skills to obtain employment, if he would get no more money than the welfare payment (let alone less)?

You might think that no major government program would ever have such a perverse set of incentives, but unfortunately that's not so.

> The main welfare program in the United States, Aid to Families with Dependent Children (AFDC), offered a 100% negative income tax throughout the 1960s, '70s, and '80s. In fact, it was even worse than that. A working family would not only lose one dollar of AFDC for every dollar earned, but they would also lose benefits such as food stamps and Medicaid. On top of that, wage earners paid positive income taxes on money they earned from work, reducing their take-home pay even further. In other words, the negative income tax was for many years typically greater than 100 percent! (Taylor 2012, 95)[5]

The everyday pragmatics of the welfare system are thorny problems.

The last major overhaul of the welfare system was in 1996 when AFDC was changed to TANF (Temporary Assistance for Needy Families). Among the most important changes were strong work requirements and a lifetime limit for cash assistance. States have considerable leeway in the details of their programs. In Illinois, for example, to receive cash benefits now the able-bodied non-working TANF participant who is not in a learning program (schooling, job training, counseling, etc.) is required to put in several hours of volunteer service weekly at food pantries, soup kitchens and other places that serve the disadvantaged. There are many people who receive food stamps who have income above that provided by TANF, but there is also an income cut-off there. When Elana's daughter recently found full-time work, her LINK card (i.e., food stamps) was limited to six months, but fortunately her medical card continues. The mere fact that there were reforms shows considerable U.S. flexibility with regard to social policy.

Part of welfare reform involved requiring recipients to participate in various learning programs. Illustrating with a personal story, a few years ago a man came into Pat's class to have her sign a form attesting to his attendance that evening so he could get his check. Tuition and books were paid through the welfare system along with a living allowance. When he found out there was to be a test he decided not to stay, but wanted her to sign anyway since he had shown up. She solved her dilemma by writing something like "Mr. What's-His-Name came to class tonight for the first time, but did not stay because we were having a test, and he was obviously not prepared." Even the most passionate advocate for the poor acknowledges that some people scam the system.

But working the system is not necessarily scamming it. Our friend Elana explains that the rules allow transferring the legal residence of a child from one family member to another, between parent and grandparent for example, in order to maximize housing subsidies. This is similar to divorced parents negotiating who gets the child deduction on their income taxes. For the poor navigating the welfare rules is a way to increase income for survival, and the intent is not much different from the way the more well-to-do navigate the tax system to minimize their tax bills.

Whether the 1996 reform was a success or not depends on what your goals are. Martin and Caminada (2011) find "welfare reform did serve to increase work participation rates, although the earnings of most individuals who left welfare were still below the poverty line, even many years after their exit" (Martin and Caminada 2011, 1). Its effect on education again depended on your point of view. On the one hand it decreased the dropout rate of teens; but on the other hand it also decreased the probability of college or high school enrollment of adults (Dave, Corman, and Reichman 2012). One other result is that although cash welfare payments were unaffected by the 2008 financial crisis and subsequent recession, the use of food stamps and other non-cash benefits increased significantly (Bitler and Hoynes, 2010).

As with education, there are considerable differences in the generosity of welfare programs depending on local conditions and preferences. Economists have found that people report significant differences in their attitudes toward welfare spending. People reduce their willingness to support welfare programs as the proportion of welfare recipients rises in a community but increase their willingness to support welfare programs as the racial composition increasingly reflects their own group. This helps explain why racially heterogeneous states have relatively low welfare benefits (Luttmer 2001). It is also generally the case that ethnic conflict is an important, and negative, determinant of local public services (Alesina, Baqir, and Easterly 1999, 1243). But Jannett and a coauthor have some tentative evidence that diversity tends to increase spending on productive municipal services in some circumstances (Highfill and O'Brien 2014). This is certainly an area for further research.

Economists argue that the government has to make and enforce rules that foster productivity and fairness. Conservatives are essentially worried about the productivity half of that equation. The columnist Byron York (August 16, 2012 Peoria *Journal* Star) spelled it out in the context of a presidential election. Conservatives are worried about the federal deficit, socialized medicine, and state's rights. "But perhaps the biggest conservative worry about a second Obama administration involves something far bigger: that after eight years of President Obama, more Americans will be dependent on government than ever before, with still more on track to become dependent in the future." As we have learned, less prosperous people rely on networks to survive. The question is to what degree that network should include the government.

Liberals are usually more comfortable with the government playing a role in providing a social safety net. In Jeffrey Sachs's *Common Wealth: Economics For a Crowded Planet* (2008, 268) the essential argument, based on international comparisons, is that "the United States does not have to accept continued high rates of poverty as the price to pay for a vibrant market economy, since social insurance can be combined with a high-productivity market economy." We will give his data later, but the basic idea is that the countries with the highest GDP per capita by his measure also have the lowest poverty rates because they are productive enough to provide the needed transfer payments.

The economy must incorporate the wisdom of both conservatives and liberals. One program that both ends of the political spectrum often support is the Earned Income Tax Credit, enacted in 1975 to offset the Social Security taxes deducted from the earnings of the working poor. Conservatives like it because it reduces the negative effect on incentives of pure welfare. To receive this tax subsidy a person must be working, contributing to the economy in that way. Liberals like it because the amount of help provided is substantial. While it was originally dwarfed by the more traditional welfare assistance programs, total expenditures are now about twice as large as the payments to families where no one is employed (Laing 2011, 263).

In this section we have worked our way through how an economy creates prosperity by investment in businesses through the financial markets and investment in education. We thought about the emergence of modern labor markets because that's where the payoff from the investment in education often comes—not to mention every business needs labor. We've concluded with a chapter on the social safety net because a modern economy is unimaginable without it.

Tip O'Neill, long-time Speaker of the House (1977–1987) had a quotation from Vice President Hubert Humphrey on his wall: "The moral test of government is how it treats those who are in the dawn of life, the children; those who are in the twilight of life, the aged; and those who are in the shadows of life—the sick, the needy and the handicapped."[6]

The next section confronts a difficult question about the social safety net: Does help really help?

NOTES

1. See for example Charles Krauthammer, September 19, 2011, Peoria *Journal Star*.

2. It seems very problematical to ask individuals to entirely manage their own "Social Security retirement accounts" or hire a financial advisor to do so. Different people starting with

the same amount to invest would emerge with different returns, but the differences would be attributable to luck rather than skill or differences in risk preferences.

3. Although we believe there are real advantages to growing up in a three generation household, young people by and large do not seem to prefer that arrangement, nor do many grandparents.

4. For shorthand the process is often called "creative destruction."

5. The preceding numerical example is also adapted from Taylor.

6. See Tip O'Neill (1987 with William Novak) *Man of the House: The Life and Political Memoirs of Speaker Tip O'Neill.*

III

Thinking Harder: Does "Help" Really Help?

Chapter Fourteen

The Wisdom of Families—Good Intentions and Unintended Consequences

We call the programs the government provides to help the impoverished and others in economic difficulty "the social safety net," a figure of speech meant to remind us that a good net catches the big fish but lets the little ones escape. A good social safety net would protect people from catastrophic events but make them cope with the minor setbacks of life themselves. It's a useful metaphor. Everyone agrees that society should help those who suffer the catastrophe of a 100 percent disability, but you should deal with a dead battery on the way to a job interview yourself. The question is what to do about all the issues and situations in between. Many economists traditionally have argued that a relatively generous social safety net reduces the incentives to work and invest. That is, it could weaken the economic foundations of prosperity enough that society can no longer afford to fulfill its major responsibilities, including helping the poor. This section takes on this question as seriously as we know how.

We believe it is a question where the wisdom of families is especially relevant. A dead battery is often the outcome of choices a person makes. If you own a car you decide how often to check and replace the battery. Society certainly expects you to make that decision and live with the consequences. But taking the same issue down to the family level, things may be a bit different. Suppose the teenager in the household has a car that is provided by family resources, but used exclusively by the teenager. What happens when the battery goes dead? Probably you go rescue the teenager wherever they are, even if it means getting up from the Thanksgiving dinner table. But suppose a dead battery becomes a continuing issue, even after family resources have been used to replace the old battery. Suppose the dead battery seems to be caused by something like playing music when the car isn't running.

That's the kind of small everyday issue families cope with all the time. From one angle raising children is navigating the transition from protecting them from the consequences of their decisions to making them deal with those consequences themselves. After you've rescued your teenager from a dead battery a couple of times, it's time to make sure something changes. As the stakes in the children's decisions get larger, many parents wrestle with how much of a family safety net to give their children. In the language of families, when the stakes are high parents sometimes ratchet up family discipline into "tough love" type solutions.

As "tough love" suggests, we now turn our attention to the question of whether the social safety net should be scaled back. We'll proceed by thinking about the way market discipline impacts the poor and the rich, and then consider the asymmetries and double standards that result in applying "tough love" to one group and not the other. Ultimately we will argue that the wisdom people learn from thinking about tough love in their own family situations can help us think about the macroeconomy.

Chapter Fifteen

Tough Love for the Poor

Together at supper one evening after a particularly trying day the director of a social agency wondered aloud to Pat about whether they had ever really helped anyone out of poverty. They do a lot to help people get through the day, week, month, but escaping poverty is more than that as she certainly knew. The question here is whether we should have special programs like those provided at the agency designed to help families at the lower end of the income distribution, or whether, in fact, these programs are counter-productive both for the families and for society. The basic idea is that we might be doing the poor a favor to reduce or eliminate most social safety net programs, i.e., impose "tough love" on the poor; this is akin to the "stop being enablers" idea in some family addiction interventions. We'll talk later about "tough love for the rich," but for now we want to give the "tough love for the poor" argument its best hearing.

The way to get someone to work hard and smart is to give them a cut of the proceeds of that work; the corollary is that someone who doesn't work as hard or as smart should get less than someone who does. When something goes awry in that equation it creates serious problems.

Everyone probably knows an example. Jannett sits next to a couple at the local minor league baseball games who used to own a HVAC vent cleaning business. Over the years she's heard how the business is going. Fairly early she heard that in addition to the couple themselves, they had their brothers working with them. That seemed to go well, but some time later for whatever reason they had to hire their nephew. The problem was that as far as anyone could tell the nephew had zero work skills and the same work ethic. (That no doubt contributed to the fact that he needed a job. . . .) The point is that if the market principle had prevailed they never would have employed the nephew, they would have made more money, and they would have had absolutely no reduction in the amount or quality of the service they provided their customers. The prevailing family rules reduced the efficiency of their business. The sad story is that they seemed to be the employer of last resort for the whole family, and eventually had to close their doors because payroll outgrew revenue. They could support themselves with the business but not their whole network, since not everyone worked as hard or smart as they did.

This couple learned that balancing family and market principles can be quite difficult. We argued in chapter 5 that wrestling with these difficult issues is a moral requirement for everyone. The tough love for the poor argument is that the only way this nephew will learn to not be a free rider is to refuse to help him in the first place. That is a hard lesson for everyone to learn. In a sense, it is learning a point of view—nobody owes you anything.

So this argument is essentially that every time you help someone you're reinforcing exactly the wrong moral. (Please remember that we're making the best case for this point of view—not that we agree with it in all situations.) One of our colleagues volunteers at an after school program which helps children with homework as well as gives them a little snack, crackers and Kool-Aid. Because of the income range of the children the program receives some government funding, but not enough to cover its actual costs. The director of the program proposed having the children bring a quarter to pay for the crackers, but the children did not think that was fair. In our way of thinking they were using the family principle. If you're at your grandmother's house (or the house of anyone in your network) and there are crackers when you are hungry, then you are welcome to them. You may have to wait for snack time, but that's true everywhere. By family rules, the crackers are to be shared if you have them. By market rules the crackers have to be paid for. The center certainly had to pay for them. Since the program itself was free in this case, the director thought it was only fair that the children should pay a small amount to help defray the expense.

The reaction of the children is not surprising. No one is born knowing food has to be paid for. How soon and how harshly they learn is the question. The "tough love" argument is that they need to learn even as children in an after school program about how markets work. Go back far enough, someone worked to pay for the crackers, either the working parent who gives the child a quarter, or the working taxpayer if the family receives government benefits.

A second argument is that people who use a network to survive and meet their most immediate needs might, in circumstances like these, begin to think of the government as a part of their network. From a market point of view, that is a real problem. With the friends and family parts of their network they understand that they get benefits sometimes but they give benefits at other times. They may think of the government, however, only as a provider of benefits. They may not be aware of any responsibilities to the government other than the normal one of being law-abiding citizens. In fact, they may become indignant at the very idea of their having any other responsibilities or at the idea of a benefit being reduced, whatever the justification.

The many aids given through non-governmental social agencies may be even more likely to be regarded as a permanent part of their living standards. Most of these agencies pride themselves on the amount of help they give, even justifying themselves through statistics that way. Where we live in Peoria, Illinois, several groups give school children backpacks stocked with supplies shortly before school starts in the fall. The executive director for the Dream Center, Andy King, said, "I don't ever want to make an announcement that we're all out of backpacks again to families" as reported by Thomas Bruch (July 29, 2012), in the Peoria *Journal Star*.[1]

Expecting this continuing stream, children may not learn to take care of what they have been given. The children expect the crayons will be replaced when they break them. Why not? They were given them before. They expect their backpacks will be replaced when they break the zippers, when they wear out the bottoms by dragging them along instead of wearing them, when they just throw them down instead of hanging them on hooks provided. If you have children you will remember that you had to teach them to take care of the things they used, that crayons, backpacks, clothes and toys, and money when they were older "didn't grow on trees." We all value what we have worked for more than gifts, except of course, when the giver is someone special to us and we know that giving it to us was special to them. Even "soup kitchen" programs find that the people who come regularly sometimes complain about the menu and the fact that seconds are not available until everyone has had their firsts. They are hungry, and it is the agency's job to feed them.

People making a tough love for the poor argument are concerned about creating "welfare generations," and they have good reason to be concerned. There really is a group of people permanently in "the housing" or "the projects" as the HUD subsidized developments are often called. Quoting from Elana again:

> Many people move to low income housing (the projects) to transition from living with parents, friends, or other family members. They are so anxious to gain independence or are just fed up with their current situations that they don't take the time to devise a plan and before they know it the projects become a permanent residence or a trap as such. Then they start to feel comfortable, complacent, and figure/decide ok, this is where I/we are and will be. These are the ones who almost never make it out. The ones who become dependent on the government, agencies, and others. The ones who don't benefit from the help and kindness of others because they have come to "expect" it. (personal communication)

Elana worries that if you lived with your mother and became a single parent, you might just expect to raise your children the same way. She estimates only 20 to 30 percent of the poor make it out of poverty, but she is determined that her grandson will be one that does.

On a more mundane level, prospering in a market environment requires learning the everyday "rules of the road." Consider tardiness as compared to getting to work on time. Suppose your extended family, living in three different apartments with four (or more) adults, shares one and a half cars. Well, they have two cars but each only runs about 75 percent of the time. Transportation to work and shopping and other essential functions is a logistical challenge; given the vagaries of real life you get used to waiting, or making others wait. A person who lives in that environment may find it difficult to get used to (or take seriously) a job that requires exact punctuality. The "dress up" clothes your network admires may be a far cry from the more professional look an employer expects. Networking on the employer's time might also be a problem.

The "tough love for the poor" argument boils down to the idea that prosperity is produced by markets; when you pay someone to not work, regardless of how that payment is justified or packaged, you are reinforcing the wrong moral. Robert Lupton in *Toxic Charity* (2011) strongly argues that "little affirms human dignity more than honest work. One of the surest ways to destroy self-worth is subsidizing the idleness of able-bodied people" (Lupton 2011, 152).

A country's ability to help the less fortunate depends on its prosperity. It is shortsighted for a country to have policies that discourage market discipline. Although some individuals would be helped by these policies, in the long run they would be even better off learning how to contribute to the economy, and if they themselves would not be better off, their children would be.

This is the tough love for the poor argument in a nutshell. We will give our evaluation of it in chapter 17. But before we do, it will be useful to think about the other side of the coin, what tough love for the rich might mean.

NOTE

1. As by reported by Lauren Zumbach (July 28, 2013) also in the Peoria *Journal Star*, the number of backpacks given away has grown from 300 to 3,000 over the "dozen years."

Chapter Sixteen

Tough Love for the Rich

For years the term goldbricking has been used to describe people loafing and not doing their fair share on the job. It started as swindling, coating ordinary bricks with gold to deceive people. In modern parlance goldbricking refers to people using the Internet at work for personal reasons, everything from shopping to watching a YouTube clip to streaming an entire movie. Staring at a computer screen gives the appearance of working without accomplishing a darn thing. In the previous chapter we told a story about a couple with an HVAC cleaning business. In a nutshell when they had to employ unproductive family members they found it hard to stay in business. In markets that is the desired outcome because it is the efficient one; a company who pays unproductive workers should not be able to survive in the long run. While in the next section we argue that there is a lot of truth to that, we can't help but observe that there seem to be a number of businesses with a nephew working in them. Even in the most avowedly market-oriented sectors of the economy it is by no means obvious that every employee carries his or her own weight.

For a second example, think about how the government affects productivity. Every economy needs a functioning government, partly to do things like keep the peace, but markets require certain additional things from the government. Property rights must be well defined and enforced. There must be neutral third party enforcement of contracts. The economy needs, in short, a well functioning civil judicial system. Thus the employees of the government who work in this area are contributing to prosperity just as much as if they produced tractors or televisions. Anyone who has ever spent time in a courthouse has no doubt watched how they operate and what the various people do. It may be ignorance on the observer's part, but sometimes courthouses look a little like a family business. Someone gets elected sheriff or appointed city manager and later various family or network members end up on the payroll. They may be nothing like the nephew of the HVAC cleaning business, but on the other hand. . . .

In a quite different example, we have a former student who worked for about six years in Chicago as a computer engineer, earning $150,000 a year at the end. Then he was abruptly laid off; his employer had found that it could outsource his function to an Indian engineer, paying that engineer about 15 percent of what the American was paid. The Indian engineer did have other costs the American one did not have: distance, time zones, misunderstandings caused by cultural differences. But as a percent of the American engineer's salary, it still made sense from the firm's point of view to outsource the position. Our former student, having learned from us the market principle, knew it was his responsibility to find other employment. He knew how to do a good job search—and did it.

When he found another position, it involved changing cities and a new salary a bit over $70,000, under half of what he was making before. From one angle he was shocked, but in talking to us about it later he said that he finally understood why competition for jobs at his firm had been so fierce the last few years. And he remembered us telling him and his class that anytime there is too great a gap between the salary you're making and your next best alternative, be on the lookout because your job may be in trouble. This is a person who was worth what he was paid when he was hired, assuming the hiring firm was doing its homework. But by the end, he was no longer worth what he was being paid.

An example, similar in some ways, different in others, concerns a factory town with a unionized workforce. Think of a town whose employment is dominated by the production facility of a single firm; for good or for ill many towns in the Northeast and Midwest states would serve as examples. Wages at the factory were determined by negotiation, and it was often the case that they depended more on national negotiations than on anything specific to that community. Communities get used to this; all too often the public school system does not excel at college preparation when a union-scale factory job pays more than many a profession requiring college. While in high school Pat's granddaughter was paid union scale at the park district skating rink for picking up small children from the ice and standing them back on their feet. She worked only a few hours a week, of course, but that job paid an hourly rate better than that for any of the (non-unionized, female) full-time support staff at our University. So what happened in all those industrial towns? Not every high school graduate got a factory job, and the next best alternative employment for those that didn't paid significantly less.

So in a sense there was a "jobs lottery" getting out of high school. Those who won got good paying factory jobs, those who lost the jobs lottery didn't. One cousin got on at the factory, another didn't. The family dynamics at many a Thanksgiving dinner table were dominated by that great divide. As with the computer engineer, if you're making considerably more than your next best alternative, some of your compensation is probably not related to your contribution. In a market sector don't be surprised if the factory eventually demands wage concessions. If your union votes down the concessions, don't be surprised when the factory closes.

There is another example of disconnect between compensation and contribution that we need to talk about. In chapter 9 we said a primary function of the financial markets is to facilitate turning household saving into investment by firms. Risk is integral to all economic matters, but to investment particularly. Financial advisors, for example, are in the business of helping households and other non-financial businesses hold their financial wealth in a way that balances risk and reward. Newspapers sometimes refer to them as stock pickers.

Between March 1988 and January 2001, *The Wall Street Journal* ran several contests pitting professional stock brokers against stocks picked by throwing four darts at a listing of stocks on the New York Stock Exchange. It turned out that "dart picks beat the pros over the 1990–2001 period both on a cumulative wealth and risk-adjusted basis. Neither dart nor pro picks beat the S&P 500 or the DJIA on a raw return basis, and both fall well behind on a risk-adjusted basis" (Adams and Cyree 2004, 40). Kahneman and his students have also studied this issue extensively. "Although professionals are able to extract a considerable amount of wealth from amateurs, few stock pickers, if any, have the skill needed to beat the market consistently, year after year" (Kahneman 2011, 214).

Kahneman's commentary is biting. Referring to the financial advice industry: "A major industry appears to be built largely on an *illusion of skill*" (italics in the original) (Kahneman 2011, 212). Further, "we know that people can maintain an unshakeable faith in any proposition, however absurd, when they are sustained by a community of like-minded believers. Given the professional culture of the financial community, it is not surprising that large numbers of individuals in that world believe themselves to be among the chosen few who can do what they believe others cannot" (Kahneman 2011, 217). The bottom line is that the major houses on Wall Street, and to some extent the financial markets in general, are "rewarding luck as if it were skill" (Kahneman 2011, 216).

On a personal note we should say that we do not advise our friends against having a financial advisor. We ourselves have them.[1] But know what you are paying for—help with transactions and record keeping and perhaps some help managing risk appropriately for circumstances. But if you have a financial advisor precisely because you know you don't know which stocks to pick to beat the market, well, neither does your financial advisor.

Among the many tasks of the well-paid chief financial officers of corporations is investing current surplus cash to obtain maximum return. A study by Kahneman and collaborators indicates CFOs have difficulty forecasting future moves in the stock market. The study's

> conclusion was straightforward: financial officers of large corporations had no clue about the short-term future of the stock market; the correlation between their estimates and the true value was slightly less than zero! When they said the market would go down, it was slightly more likely than not that it would go up. These findings are not surprising. The truly bad news is that the CFOs did not appear to know that their forecasts were worthless. (Kahneman 2011, 261)[2]

If part of their pay is for forecasting, the question is whether they are a greater relative drag on their employer than the nephew hired by the owners of the HVAC cleaning business.

And if CFOs are well paid, chief executive officers are truly rewarded like princes. There is an enormous literature on the relationship between CEO characteristics and a business's overall performance. In a world of perfect markets, successful firms would be managed by good CEOs, unsuccessful firms by bad ones. On the other hand, if the leadership skills of CEOs are utterly unrelated to firm performance, then by the laws of chance, a successful firm would be led by a good CEO 50 percent of the time and a bad CEO 50 percent of the time. In Kahneman's view a generous estimate is that 60 percent of successful firms are led by strong CEOs, so there is some correlation, but not as much as you might expect (Kahneman 2011, 205). The corollary is that many firms perform well in spite of rather than because of the efforts of their CEO. That wouldn't be all bad if CEO compensation structure distinguished between firm performance and CEO performance, but usually that attempt isn't even made. It is not even self-evident that CEO compensation in general reflects firm performance (Stiglitz 2012, 42 and 316). Many CEO employment contracts are written so that even if they are fired for poor firm performance they get a "golden parachute" which may be less than their regular pay, but is still many multiples of the income of an average American by any measure. That's the rub.

In 2011 the median CEO compensation for the S&P 500 was $9.6 million, meaning half of them made more than that, as reported by Matt Krantz and Barbara Hansen (March 31, 2012) in *USA Today*. CEOs make as much as 300 times the average pay of a production worker as reported by Katrina vanden Heuvel (August 31, 2011) in *The Nation*. A working person trying to scare up enough money to register their children in school tomorrow, let alone get the school supplies list, might be forgiven for wondering just what those CEOs did to deserve all that money. The 18,000 persons threatened with job loss with the closing of Hostess Brands Inc. in 2012 might have wondered why the bankruptcy court approved $1.8 million for bonuses for the company executives conducting the liquidation process, that is, selling its iconic brands, Twinkies and Ding Dongs.

The 2008 financial crisis, subsequent recession, and weak recovery had profound effects on most of us. It was caused by the problems in the financial sector.[3] Executives in the financial sector might be the most egregious examples of goldbricking in the country. Financial markets are crucial to the economy; when they misfire the recessions caused are the deepest and most difficult to recover from (Cerra and Saxena 2008). If the principle that reward follows contribution were applied to the financial market executives, it would follow that their compensation would be vastly reduced after the crisis. We might also argue that their compensation should not return to pre-crisis levels until some macroeconomic indicators also recover, employment and work force participation rates perhaps. It might even require that they repay some compensation they got during the financial bubbles in the run-up to the crisis.

To say these things have not generally happened is an understatement. Technically this is often because of the contracts executives had, and the notion that contracts must in all fairness always be honored. Joseph Stiglitz, an Obama advisor himself, points out the absurdity of an Obama administration official who said "with a straight face, that it was necessary to honor AIG bonuses, even for the officials who had led the company to need a $150 billion bailout, because of the sanctity of contracts; minutes later he could admonish autoworkers to accept a revision of their contract that would have lowered their compensation enormously" (2012, 67). Both the contracts of the AIG executives and the contracts of the union workers were designed to short-circuit market discipline. Sometimes society is better off taking a break from market discipline, sometimes not—but those arguments have to be made carefully and fairly. We will turn to these matters in chapters 22 and 23.

The moral hazards of deposit insurance, "too big to fail" etc., have been recognized by economists for decades. Following the Great Depression the government created a set of financial market regulations that were reasonably functional for perhaps fifty years. Some of the regulations were repealed or allowed to lapse; some were made irrelevant by the globalization of financial markets. While family wisdom might contribute to banks being more prudent, unfortunately we don't see it as contributing much of substance to the discussion of what the future regulatory environment of "too big to fail" institutions needs to look like.

There is a disparity in how the rich in society are treated as compared to the way the middle and lower classes are treated (or the upper-middle class for that matter). Acemoglu, whom we have quoted before, said in an interview that the financial crisis was

> an outcome of the political processes that have removed all of the regulations in finance, and so created the platform for 40 percent of U.S. corporate profits to be in the financial sector—which is just an amazing number. . . . And that's for a sector that doesn't use much capital, so it went to a very few, 20,000 or so people, in a very unequal way—especially in the form of year-end bonuses. They were amazingly overrepresented in the top 0.1 percent of the income distribution. . . . So it could well be that a political process that responded not to the *bottom* of the income distribution, but to the lobbying, financial and expertise power of the *very top* of the income distribution might have been responsible. (Clement 2011, 24–25; italics in the original)

The financial crisis was also a vivid reminder that trusting experts to guide us through significant macroeconomic uncertainties is problematic. We quote Kahneman again: "One of the lessons of the financial crisis that led to the Great Recession is that there are periods in which competition, among experts and among organizations, creates powerful forces that favor a collective blindness to risk and uncertainty" (Kahneman 2011, 262). Even worse, experts, financial advisors, pundits on television, and unfortunately many of the rest of us "get credit for prescience that they do not deserve. . . . [The false implication is] that the world is more knowable than it is. It helps perpetuate a pernicious illusion" (Kahneman 2011, 201).

Anyone who seriously tackles the question of whether outcomes correlate well with contributions has to take uncertainty, risk, and thus luck into account. When you don't know what will happen to the economy you have to guess, and the eventual outcome depends both on the quality of the guess and luck. This is true for individual executives and for the businesses where they work (Kahneman 2011, 200–201). To his credit Bill Gates, of Microsoft fame, forthrightly says so. "I had a better exposure to software development at a young age than I think anyone did in that period of time, and all because of an incredibly lucky series of events" (Gladwell 2008, 55).

For another kind of example, Tagg Romney went into the private equity business and founded Solamere with $10 million in seed money from his family and with his father's finance chairman as a partner. According to Michael Luo and Julie Creswell of *The New York Times* (April 30, 2012), sixty-four investors put in $244 million even though Tagg Romney had no prior experience in private equity. Tagg Romney has stated, "Our relationships with people got us in the door, but that did not get us investors."

Figuring out when goldbricking is happening is sometimes easy, but in an uncertain world it is often quite difficult since market outcomes depend on both skill and luck. We are not necessarily arguing that there is more goldbricking at the upper reaches of the income distribution than at the middle or the bottom. But it is not self-evident that there is less either. For example, whatever your personal views are of year-end bonuses in the financial sector, for the most part there is nothing illegal going on.[4] Goldbricking is a kind of theft which is not illegal.

However we need to acknowledge briefly that, unfortunately, we also have our share of thieves who are lawbreakers. On December 10, 2008, Mark and Andrew Madoff reported to federal authorities that their father, the founder of Bernard L. Madoff Investment Securities and the former non-executive chairman of the NASDAQ stock market, had been running an investment Ponzi scheme—the largest in history. Although the story is well known in outline, the Wikipedia article still makes fascinating reading. Perhaps less well known, it turns out that the largest beneficiary of the scheme was not Madoff, but rather Jeffry Picower, a lawyer and accountant. Clicking over to read his entry you will see he had been in trouble with the SEC for inadequate disclosure and with the IRS for a tax shelter scheme, and he had been chairman of the board of a corporation which falsified financial statements. Although Wall Street had been skeptical of Madoff's returns (none of the major Wall Street houses would invest with him nor would the derivative firms trade with him), J.P. Morgan Chase & Co. also benefited from the Madoff's Ponzi scheme through legitimate interest and fees of about $1.5 billion. As troubling as the scandal itself is, many find it even more troubling that the Securities and Exchange Commission evidently missed six separate occasions to detect the fraud, one as early as 2001–2002.

The largest bankruptcy in U.S. history was of Lehman Brothers, the country's fourth largest investment bank when it failed in 2008; this bankruptcy was caused partly by (and a cause of) the 2008 financial crisis and partly by dicey accounting gimmicks as was the earlier bankruptcy of Enron, Wikipedia's poster child of "willful corporate fraud and corruption." (What do you want to bet that phrase has shown up in hundreds of school reports?) The frauds of these businesses, and others we haven't mentioned, were efforts to manipulate stock prices, and people got unbelievably rich playing these games. An impartial observer could not help but conclude that the financial markets are complicit in spectacular fraud in our society.

Those who follow the news about the financial markets could be forgiven for wondering how it all adds up. People do in fact get paid breathtaking sums at least some part of which is attributable to luck, and in a few headline cases, theft. It might be possible to regulate financial markets in such a way that compensation better matches contributions to the economy, but so far we haven't found a magic bullet. We are also aware that the motives of many professionals in the financial markets mirror ours, to make a contribution to the world. Pat has a friend who gave up her job as a real estate agent two weeks after getting her license because she believed it was immoral to try to sell houses to people who couldn't afford them. Finally, financial market innovations can be good and should be encouraged when they facilitate market functioning.[5]

The challenge to regulate the economy is dealt with most immediately by politicians which leaves them in a terrible box. On the one hand, they may well know that the rich were lucky—smart and hard working—but also lucky; nevertheless they still need money to fund their political campaigns. The entire lifetime earnings of a college teacher or two would be invisible in the coffers of a presidential candidate. Whether we like it or not there is a sense in which money is the measure of many things in society. The opinions of rich people count more with many politicians than do those of the poor.

We will conclude this chapter by thinking for a moment about what it would mean to apply tough love to the rich. There are some fundamental asymmetries between tough love for the rich and tough love for the poor—even setting aside the fairness issues for a moment which we will tackle head on in the next chapter.

If you buy the tough love for the poor argument, no other action is required. The argument is precisely a rationale for doing nothing. But tough love for the rich requires that we take unearned money away from them. That is relatively easy in the cases of theft or outright fraud. The perpetrator pays restitution and a fine. But usually things are not so simple. It may be that part of a person's income is earned and part is not. The problem then is to figure out how much is unearned—that is, how much was a reward for being lucky as compared to a reward for hard work and good decision making.

One of our economist friends frequently reminds us that the market cannot distinguish between working hard and smart and simple good luck. When dealing with strangers it is next to impossible to gauge how much of a firm's success, for example, was due to the smart decisions of the CEO and his leadership team. But just because the market does not easily decide something does not mean that human beings can't make some judgments; it just makes it much harder. In practice the government usually has to get involved. You could imagine a government bureaucracy making those decisions and enforcing them. The difficulties we see in making that workable lead us to suggest that it might be more realistic to simply have a progressive income tax. That is, you might be willing to assume that anyone who earns a very large income has had at least some good luck. The progressive income tax would be taxing away some of the rewards of that luck. Robert Frank even argues that the rich are in favor of such a tax because they realize high status is a market good that has to be paid for like any other (Frank 1985, 112 ff). That is, the rich might think of progressive taxes as a kind of self-imposed tough love, requiring them to do what they want to do. (Pat has her doubts.) We'll think more about this possibility later.

Another asymmetry concerns the size of the rewards for bad behavior.[6] Earlier in this chapter we mentioned that the median CEO compensation in 2011 for an S&P 500 company was $9.6 million; 2.5 percent of $9.6 million is $240,000. For a basis of comparison we Googled recent headlines of "welfare fraud" and found individuals were alleged to have stolen amounts like $5,475, $150,000, $240,000, $150,839, and $135,000. Compare these two sets of numbers, setting aside the point that the welfare fraud may well have been over many years, upwards of twenty in some cases, and that CEO compensation is for a single year. About 2.5 percent of the median CEO compensation is the same order of magnitude as the largest of these welfare fraud amounts. So if about 2.5 percent of the CEO compensation was a reward for luck or shaky accounting then it would be about the same as the amount stolen by the welfare thief. Of course, if more than 2.5 percent of the CEO compensation is based on luck or gray-economy transactions, then the economy is rewarding the CEO more than the welfare cheat for similar behavior.

A third asymmetry concerns the stakes for the rest of us. Someone cheating on her welfare doesn't cost thousands of jobs or decimate anybody's retirement hopes. Bad decisions by the management team of any Fortune 500 company have major consequences for their employees, customers, and investors. All the welfare cheats in the world will not crash the world economy. But there is no doubt that the 2008 financial crisis was caused by the financial sector, and there is no doubt that at least the top income earners in the industry were either negligent, extremely lucky, or expert in getting the system set up to their advantage, as for example, in the enforcement of contracts.

As Jannett's mother would say, we have to be careful not to strain the gnats but swallow the flies.

NOTES

1. For examples of perfectly sensible financial advice please see Carl Richards (2012) *The Behavior Gap: Simple Ways to Stop Doing Dumb Things with Money* or Larry E. Swedroe (2011) *The Quest for Alpha: The Holy Grail of Investing*.
2. The details of this and the next study are fascinating. We recommend reading Kahneman's account.
3. This is not the place for a general discussion of the causes of the crisis. Some references we have found particularly helpful are by Bethany McLean and Joe Nocera (2010) and Gorton and Metrick (2012).
4. If no laws have been broken, then the problems must be systemic. In chapters 18 to 22, we will argue that institutions need to be improved.
5. Robert Shiller (2012, 235) for example, has some interesting ideas about the democratization and humanization of finance.
6. For some eye-popping comparisons of the size of damages that come from white collar crime as compared to blue collar crime see Ariely (2008, 195–96). To mention just one example, the losses from all robberies in the United States in 2004 was about $525 million while the

losses from employee theft and fraud was about $600 billion. Yes, that's billions as compared to millions.

Chapter Seventeen

The Wisdom of Families— Avoiding Double Standards

Real families grapple with how to relate contribution and reward all the time. You know children need to learn that reward follows contribution, and many of us try to help them start making that connection. Pat's brother was the baseball coach for his young son's park district team. The contribution he wanted from his players was for them to swing the bat. Don't just stand there and take balls to get a walk. Try. So on his team you got a stick of gum if you swung—no swing, no gum.

Unfortunately children also learn that sometimes the connection between the contribution and the reward is not so clear. A friend gives an example of two sports teams that her son is on. On the basketball team the coach sets up clear rules that relate things like missing practice to minutes played. Contribution is defined as working hard in practice and abiding by certain team rules. The reward is playing, satisfying the kids' natural desire to play in the game. On the tennis team, on the other hand, although the coach is passionately devoted to the welfare of "her kids," the rules are hard for the kids and their parents to figure out. Neither the children nor the parents are sure about what governs who gets which slot in the seeding. So there is lots of parental carping about it and efforts to lobby the coach for better treatment for their sons.

Tough love is good when it is applied fairly. In a sports context it gets good performances. But when only the less favored kids are punished by not getting to play when they break a rule, both the favored and the less-favored get the wrong message. A kid starts games because her dad is best friends with the coach when a much better player sits on the bench, even though, for example, both kids skipped the same required practice and broke the same team rules. We've all seen someone rewarded who has not made a commensurate contribution. The point for our larger project is that it is hypocritical and wrong to apply "tough love" arguments to the poor and not the rich.

Everyone is subject to the vagaries of fortune and everyone makes mistakes. Consider a twenty-something who makes a rather substantial mistake and gets a felony conviction on his record. Is he thereby sentenced to a reduced ability to earn a living the rest of his life? The answer to that depends on his social class. Much of the challenge of parenting adult children in their twenties for the middle and upper classes turns on this very issue, and often significant family resources are devoted to helping the child recover from such a mistake. We don't mean to imply that the help is always financial—the challenge for wise parents is to find the best help for that particular child. In the education chapter, we cited Paul Tough's argument that for the prosperous the educational system is designed to help children recover from their mistakes. The point is that many a middle or upper class person survives and prospers after a rather significant mistake.

The poor are often much less able to recover from such a mistake. They may not get the same support from their educational institutions. Their parents care as much but they can't do as much because they are without the resources to help the children recover. Our essential argument is that it is unfair and immoral to say the poor have to live with the consequences of their bad decisions when considerable numbers of higher income people get a hand up in recovering.

From what we have seen, families operating at their best are quite wise about the use of tough love. Even for adult children with a history of difficulty, who have made mistakes, we notice families usually do not resort to tough love until all other possibilities have been exhausted. Essentially all of the adults involved have to agree with a tough love solution. Two or three or four parents, as many grandparents as are involved in the child's life, sometimes aunts and uncles or family friends as close as family—all have to agree with the solution or it won't work. The child will pragmatically go live with whichever adult doesn't agree—negating the whole effort to force the child to stand on his or her own. People who have learned the hard way in their own families about tough love will be wise in its application to strangers. It's an extreme answer to be used in only the most extreme circumstances. It's not the first response to any issue that arises. The wisdom of families is a guide for society. The toughest level of discipline, family or market, should be applied fairly. Discipline for functional adults is self-discipline, with a wry touch of self-knowledge.

At the end of the last section we stated our belief that in a tempered and humane economy we individually and collectively have a moral responsibility to help those in need. This section, to answer the question posed by its title, argues that finding ways to really help anyone requires great wisdom—

but it is possible. One of the larger themes of this book is that the source of the necessary wisdom is what we have learned in our families, both by precept and experience. The larger economy-wide help we provide others, especially the design philosophy of such programs, is a subject we return to in chapter 22. But first, having demonstrated that rewards in the economy are not always just or fair, we need to think about the wisdom of an economy that relies substantially on markets. If the market principle that reward follows contribution is often broken in real life, might it not be better to just dispense with the pretense and move on? We next investigate that question.

IV

Prosperity is an Enormous Achievement

Chapter Eighteen

Warts and All, We Are a Big Rich Country

We need to take an unblinking look at the U.S. economy. One child in five lives in poverty. In 2012 15 percent of the U.S. population lived in poverty, 46.5 million people.[1] The unemployment rate hovers above 6 percent. Just as worrisome is the number of workers who have not recently looked for a job because they lack transportation, are in poor health, are "discouraged" having looked unsuccessfully for a job for a long time, and similar reasons; as late 2013 turned to 2014 there were upwards of two and a half million such persons. Some people wonder whether the government debt created by our responses to the 2008 financial crisis will cause problems for us down the road.

However, to judge how the United States is doing, we should compare ourselves not to a perfect world but to what has been achieved at other times and in other places. The average annual increase in real gross domestic product (GDP) for the United States since 1930 is between 2.5 percent and 3.5 percent a year, even taking into account some episodes of inflation, the Great Depression, and the 2008 financial crisis. We are now richer than we have ever been in the past.

Table 18.1 gives 2013 GDP per capita for selected countries, using purchasing power parity computed by the International Monetary Fund as the basis for comparison. Here we are comparing prosperity geographically rather than over time.

In looking at this data we want to quickly say that the point is not that the United States has the highest per capita GDP. These rankings depend on how the international comparisons are done, and later we report some results by Jeffrey Sachs putting the United States behind the Scandinavian countries. In fact, although our examples throughout the book are taken from the United

Table 18.1. GDP and Population, Selected Countries, 2013

Country	GDP per Capita[a]	Population[b]
United States	52,839	317
Canada	43,146	35
Scandinavia	42,016	26
Germany	39,468	82
United Kingdom	37,299	64
Japan	37,135	127
France	35,680	64
Europe[c]	35,196	416
Euro Area	34,272	332
Russia	18,083	141
Botswana	16,353	2
Mexico	15,608	118
Brazil	12,118	200
China	9,828	1,361
Indonesia	5,182	248
India	3,991	1,243
Pakistan	3,144	183
Nigeria	2,827	169
Bangladesh	2,083	156

[a] International Monetary Fund, World Economic Outlook Database, October 2013; Estimates, in International Dollars.
[b] International Monetary Fund, World Economic Outlook Database, October 2013; Estimates, in Millions.
[c] Europe is the Euro Area, Scandinavia, and the United Kingdom.

States, our basic argument could be made for many countries in the world, certainly any down through the Euro Area in the table.[2] Many countries are somewhere on the path toward becoming modern prosperous economies—the United States is certainly not unique in that respect.

Figure 18.1 focuses on both GDP and population for a selection of countries from the table. The United States and Europe (here defined as the combination of the Euro Area, the United Kingdom, and the Scandinavian countries) have virtually the same GDP, and are both large in population.[3] Per capita GDP is shown on the diagram by the slope of a ray from the origin because GDP is on the vertical axis and population on the horizontal axis. The steeper the ray the higher the per capita GDP. So since the United States and Europe have about the same GDP but Europe has a somewhat larger population than the United States, its per capita production is somewhat smaller than that of the United States. Nevertheless, both areas have achieved something special in world history; they have large populations and high GDP per capita.

Table 18.1 also contains the dozen largest countries in the world in terms of population. Besides the United States and Europe, Japan is the only one with a GDP per capita in the top part of the table—in fact it is very similar to Europe's. China has a GDP that is approaching that of Europe and the United States, but with a population that is four times as large its GDP per capita is about a fourth that of the United States. India's population is only moderately less than China's but it has a much smaller GDP and thus a still smaller GDP per capita. A few other countries are in the figure and table for comparison purposes.

In the United States many observers believe special attention should be paid to the fortunes of the middle class. There are many ways to measure what it means to be middle class. Figures 18.2 and 18.3 use definitions and data from Alan Krueger in a talk given to the Center for American Progress (2012), when he was Chairman of Obama's Council of Economic Advisors.[4]

For an easy way to understand figure 18.2, suppose the median household income in the United States were $50,000. Then "middle class households" would be those with incomes between $25,000 and $75,000. The height of the bars gives the proportion of all households that meet this definition of middle class. Decade by decade there has been a modest decline in the proportion of households that are middle class by this definition. Now fewer

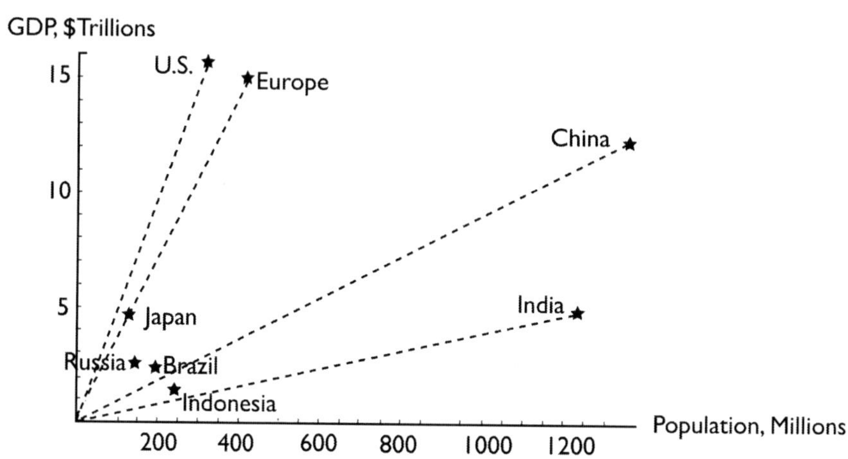

Figure 18.1. GDP and Population, Selected Countries, 2013

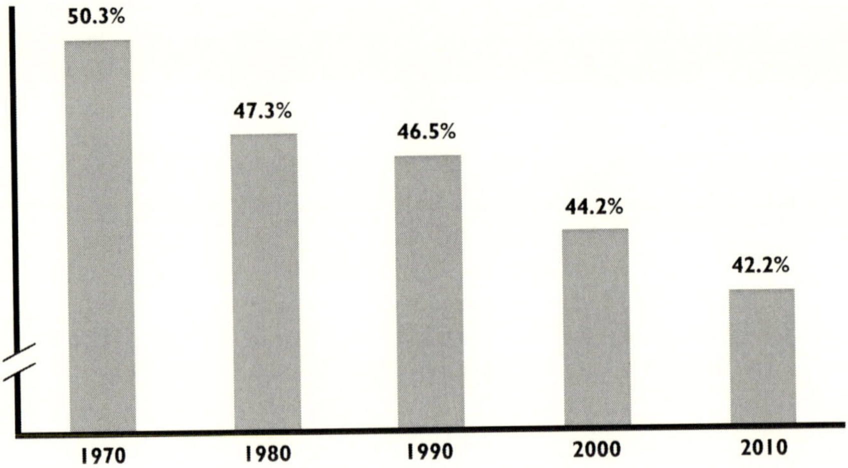

Figure 18.2. Percent of U.S. Households with Annual Income within 50 Percent of Median

than half of us are, and the proportion is decreasing not increasing, even though income for all groups has grown since 1970, as we see in figure 18.3.

Since the 1970s we've had our ups and downs economically. One cumulative measure is growth in after-tax income after adjusting for inflation. If you rank order households from poorest to richest, and divide the list into fifths, you get the information shown in figure 18.3, data again taken from Krueger (2012).[5]

Notice that the data ends in 2007, and thus does not take the 2008 crisis and subsequent recession into account. (The inequality is worse now but to the extent that the increased inequality is caused by the crisis and recession, recovery may help. Thus we focus on the interval up to the crisis.) In something under thirty years the poorest quintile's income went up by 18 percent, with the growth rates increasing for each quintile at each step. The highest quintile went up by about 65 percent, when you exclude the top 1 percent from that group. As shown, the top 1 percent saw a 278 percent increase in after-tax real income. These numbers can be hard to wrap your head around. Krueger says one way to see it is that "the *increase* in the share of income going to the top 1 percent over this period exceeds the *total* amount of income that the entire bottom 40 percent of households receives" (2012, italics not in the original).

In section VI we will talk more about technological improvements as one source of our prosperity. But when combined with globalization, it creates stress for the middle and lower ranges of the income distribution, with most economists putting somewhat more emphasis on technology than globaliza-

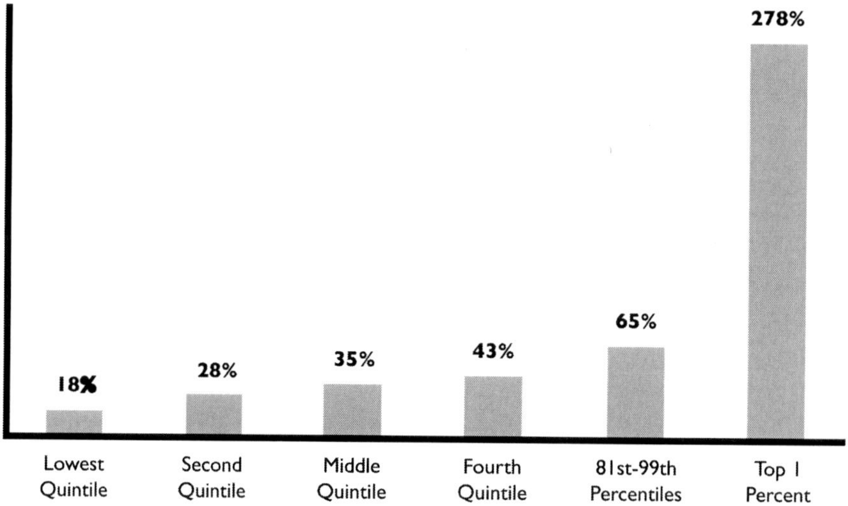

Figure 18.3. Growth in U.S. Real After-Tax Income, 1979–2007

tion. Here we simply want to make the point that for people on the bottom on the income distribution looking up, the fewer the middle class jobs there are the more investment required to get one.[6] A shrinking middle class does not relieve the middle class of its responsibilities to the poor, but it does make life tougher for both the poor and the middle class.

At this point we want to pause and look again at the title of this chapter. No one familiar with the U.S. economy would deny that we have real problems. We've just talked about some huge ones. The previous section was stuffed with them; we've mentioned both drug dealers and Ponzi schemes. Feige and Cebula (2011) have estimated that 18–19 percent of reportable income is not actually reported to the IRS. The income and GDP data we've talked about in this chapter come from the National Income Accounting system—which doesn't count drug deals, or under the table payments, or any other transaction the government isn't privy to. Mark Koba, senior CNBC editor (April 24, 2013), reports that this "underground economy" is about $2 trillion. The "above-ground" U.S. GDP is approaching $16.8 trillion. Thus the underground economic activity is a substantial portion of all economic activity, perhaps more than 10 percent. The official data, therefore, actually underestimates the prosperity of the country. That's evidence we are a rich country; it's also evidence that we have problems.

It has been argued that the government's ignorance of individual market transactions is not itself an important issue. Remember the basic market principle that reward follows contribution; customers, not the government, decide the value of a particular contribution—service or product. Certainly if the microwave you buy isn't worth it for whatever reason, take it back. If enough people take back a company's products it will go out of business. It's the same thing if you don't approve of a company's environmental or employment practices, then just don't buy from them. If enough people do the same that company is out of business as well. This is what economists mean when we say markets are self-regulating or self-monitoring. They often are, but not always.

There are two issues. The first is that in the modern world few people are capable of monitoring the performance and safety of electrical or pharmaceutical products, for example. The second issue is that even when customers can effectively monitor the quality of a product, the companies do not always live up to their side of the bargain. Suppose the store doesn't take the inadequate microwave back? Or more substantively, suppose a flawed pharmaceutical causes a permanent health issue that the firm refuses to take responsibility for. The point is that even when customers are quite vigilant in their monitoring, you still need a legal system for the neutral third-party enforcement of contracts. We need a government, and governments have to be paid for. We need taxes, and it's in everyone's best interest that their neighbors pay their fair share of those taxes. You can look at the IRS as citizens outsourcing the function of monitoring their neighbors' tax contributions.

The U.S. economy is quite prosperous, it has problems, and it needs a government. In the next section we will think more about what that government should and should not do to temper the economy. But before we do that, in this data-rich chapter we will present some numbers from Jeffrey Sachs, an influential development economist, that relate prosperity, technology, and government spending. He does an international comparison among prosperous countries. By his reckoning, the countries with the highest per capita GDP are Denmark, Finland, Norway, and Sweden; he calls these the "social welfare" group. The second highest group is Australia, Canada, Ireland, New Zealand, the United Kingdom, and the United States, the "free-market" group. The third highest in terms of per capita income is Austria, Belgium, France, Germany, Italy, and the Netherlands, the "mixed" market economy group (Sachs 2008, 258).[7] Notice that *all* of these countries are democratic, giving individuals the freedom to innovate and experiment, a subject we will return to in subsequent chapters.

The average ratio of government spending to GDP for these three groups was 52 percent, 38 percent, and 49 percent respectively in the early 2000s when the study was done (Sachs 2008, 259).[8] The average ratio of government social spending to GDP for the three groups was about 27 percent, 17 percent, and 26 percent respectively, or about half of total government spending for all groups (Sachs 2008, 260).[9] For comparison purposes, the ratio of government social spending to GDP for the United States was about 15 percent, slightly below the average for the free-market group. The richest group of countries, the social welfare group, had the highest overall government spending and the highest social government spending. Perhaps not surprisingly, by three separate measures they had the least poverty and inequality (Sachs 2008, 261).[10] The second richest group of countries, the free-market group, had the lowest government and social spending and, again not surprisingly, the most poverty and inequality. The mixed economy group takes the middle in all three measures.

The market is either half or more than half of economic activity as measured by GDP; at the same time government spending in general and spending on social insurance and education in particular are large parts of all prosperous economies. A relatively generous social insurance program does not sentence a society to low economic prosperity. In fact, the data suggest the opposite of that. The explanation is innovation. Spending on research and development (R&D as a percent of GDP) in the high income social welfare countries was higher than in the comparison groups, 3.0 percent as compared to 1.8 percent and 2.0 percent respectively (Sachs 2008, 263).[11] This data is the empirical foundation for our argument about innovation in a humane economy in chapter 25.

The economic evidence suggests that markets have to be an integral part of any economy with widespread prosperity. We've touched on the basic numbers in this chapter—the "what" part of the evidence. The next chapter takes up the "why."

NOTES

1. For the poverty rate: U.S. Census Bureau, Current Population Survey, 2013 Annual Social and Economic Supplement, POV01.

For the unemployment rate: U.S. Bureau of Labor Statistics, Employment Situation, Table A-1.

For the number of workers marginally attached to the labor force: U.S. Bureau of Labor Statistics, Employment Situation, Table A-16.

2. Although omitted from our table, there are many other examples from around the world: virtually any country in Europe, Korea, Australia, Singapore, Israel, and so forth.

3. The United Kingdom is, of course, a part of the European Union but not the Euro Area; Finland is a part of the Euro Area and Scandinavia.

4. The data are Council of Economic Advisor's calculations from the Current Population Survey.

5. The data are Council of Economic Advisor's calculations from the Congressional Budget Office.

6. We will touch on political issues only in passing from time to time. For a good summary of those see Stiglitz (2012). Whether you agree with his political ideas or not (and frankly we hate some of them), he frames the issues well and is generally reliable in his use of data.

7. It goes without saying that some of these countries could be classified differently, particularly the Netherlands which is in many ways a social-welfare country.

8. The data is for 2004.

9. The data is for 2001.
10. The data is for 2004.
11. The data is for 2003.

Chapter Nineteen

Inclusive vs. Extractive Institutions—Thinking Globally

The primary goal of this chapter is to understand why markets are always a part of long-term widespread prosperity. We'll use economic history around the world as our way to think about this issue, and doing so will take us out of the United States. We will also think briefly about a few other issues of globalization. After this chapter we'll again focus primarily on the U.S. economy.

In the modern world the relative prosperity of economies has not been constant. Some countries that were poor in 1900 are prosperous now, and some that were prosperous then have retreated to the middle of the pack. While there are no examples of countries achieving long-term widespread prosperity without a significant market component, in the relatively recent past there are some countries that made great economic progress through technological improvement without either democracy or the appropriate use of markets.[1] To get a handle on all that, it will be helpful to distinguish between "inclusive" and "extractive" institutions (whether economic, political, or both) as introduced by Daron Acemoglu and James Robinson (2012).

Think about all the countries that were colonies of some European country at some time in their history. The vast majority of those that are prosperous now were quite poor when colonized. When the colonists came to a poor country they had to do the work themselves to create a functioning economy, and they designed the institutions to support that, with private property rights and government decision making that included the workers, not just a de facto aristocracy. Rich countries have inclusive institutions. Your prosperity is not determined solely by the social class of your parents; you can work hard and better yourself.

Extractive institutions, on the other hand, are enemies of prosperity. As heartbreaking and ironic as it is, when colonizers came to a country that was wealthy in pre-colonial times they designed the institutions to extract the existing wealth from the indigenous population. Most countries in Latin America will do for examples. The colonizers much preferred rich colonies of course. Bluntly, if they could get away with it, the colonizers forced the indigenous population to work on plantations or mine the colony's natural resources while giving them subsistence rations or less.

People that live in prosperous inclusive countries are not always aware that most people do not live under similar circumstances. Unfortunately, countries dominated by extractive institutions are the norm, not the exception. That was true in the past and it is true today (Acemoglu and Robinson 2012, 431). The rich and powerful of any country prefer a political and economic system that has the population working and the privileged elite getting the rewards.

The real despair is for failed nation states whose governments do not provide the most important and basic function—law and order and a workable justice system. The global community can do little for such countries; they will be torn by violence and some form of civil war. As reported by Joe Kita (December 2, 2012) in *Parade*, Howard G. Buffett, whose foundation gives tens of millions of dollars each year to increase food production, believes we will be able to eliminate hunger in the United States but doubts it can be done worldwide because of "conflicts and infrastructure challenges." The United Nations has not been successful in preventing these wars.[2]

But many countries are in a kind of middle ground—they are not failed nation states, but neither are they democracies. Some of these countries dominated by extractive institutions can have eras, perhaps as long as fifty years, of economic growth and increasing prosperity. This is true especially when they are poor to start with and can grow by simply copying technology from elsewhere (e.g., Argentina before 1900, the Soviet Union before 1980). As Sachs points out technology is "nonrival," so that the businesses in any country can adopt it (Sachs 2008, 205). Readers particularly interested in the relationship of technology to economic development might look at Sachs's "Climbing the Ladder of Development" (Sachs 2008, 222).

But such countries will not continue to grow. Developing new technologies is a far cry from copying existing technologies. It requires a lot more than math and science, more than developing the institutions of higher education that train mathematicians, scientists, and engineers. Acemoglu and Robinson remind us that institutions matter.

> Sustained economic growth requires innovation, and innovation cannot be decoupled from creative destruction, which replaces the old with the new in the economic realm and also destabilizes established power relations in poli-

> tics. . . . The ability of those who dominate extractive institutions to benefit greatly at the expense of the rest of society implies that political power under extractive institutions is highly coveted, making many groups and individuals fight to obtain it. (Acemoglu and Robinson 2012, 430)

So far no country with extractive institutions has gained more than "middle-income" status; they raise themselves from poverty to middle-income but get stuck there or even fall back. They do not develop the institutions that support markets. They may also have a political system that is not democratic. Amartya Sen has argued that famines are much less likely in a democracy because a free press and an active opposition political party serve as a kind of early-warning system. Governments will react to potential famines in appropriate ways when political necessity forces them to. A more recent economist, Tyler Cowen, argues that famines are caused by a "lack of wealth, lack of infrastructure, some bad government policies, and also lack of democracy. The countries where there are famines are always countries that do not build their food institutions on top of a well-functioning agribusiness platform" (Cowen 2012, 150).[3] That well-functioning agribusiness platform requires markets and inclusive institutions.

As for avoiding famine in the first place, Cowen reminds us that technological progress in agriculture is basically the story. In a book addressed to prosperous United States and Western European readers he says:

> This productivity slowdown is by far the most important food problem in the world today and yet you hardly ever hear foodies talk about it. We, as foodies, are too often overly concerned about our own consumption patterns and we lose sight of the bigger picture. For all of its altruistic cloaking, maybe that's a kind of narcissism. We focus on possible mistakes of [the European] commission—eating asparagus that was flown in—and don't spend enough time worrying about unseen omissions, in other words what doesn't happen, which in this case means slower technological progress. (Cowen 2012, 153)

He also reminds us that agricultural subsidies in the United States and Western European countries have the effect of driving food producers out of business in poor countries, making it harder for those countries to avoid famine in times of stress.[4] However, targeted subsidies might be one driver, albeit an inefficient one, of the very technological progress that brings closer the goal of eliminating world hunger. These issues are not simple.

That we ourselves live in a prosperous country is something for which we are grateful. The fact that our institutions are inclusive rather than extractive should be understood to be an enormous achievement. That was not achieved at a single blow; parts of the U.S. south only developed something like inclusive institutions after the civil rights movement of the 1950s-1960s. Acemoglu and Robinson would be the first to remind us that replacing extractive institutions with inclusive ones is "neither automatic nor easy. . . . Some luck is key, because history always unfolds in a contingent way" (Acemoglu and Robinson 2012, 427).

In a spirit of cautious optimism we recommend that you read about the country of Botswana. When it became independent from Great Britain in 1966 it had "twelve kilometers of paved roads, twenty-two citizens who had graduated from university, and one hundred from secondary school. To top it all off, it was almost completely surrounded by the white regimes of South Africa, Namibia, and Rhodesia, all of which were hostile to independent African countries run by blacks" (Acemoglu and Robinson 2012, 409). But Botswana has transformed itself from being arguably the poorest country in the world in 1966 to being a middle income country, comparable to the best in Latin America such as Costa Rica or the eastern European countries of Estonia and Hungary. How? Through a combination of courageous leadership and good fortune, it developed the humane economy and pluralistic democracy necessary for prosperity.

Another cause for cautious optimism is the microfinance movement. One of the original microlending institutions, the Grameen Bank, was founded almost by accident by Muhammad Yunus, an economics professor at Chittagong University in Bangladesh. Women making handicrafts were in virtual slavery to moneylenders for the almost trivial sums needed to buy supplies. In his first program, the total borrowing of the forty-two women in Jobra Bangladesh amounted to less than the taka equivalent of $27.[5] These programs are often differentially targeted at women, which improves their outcomes. In the context of an article about the education of girls, Mary Sanchez (October 25, 2012) of the Peoria *Journal Star* says the following:

> According to some microlending experts, when non-governmental organizations provide new access to money to men, they tend to spend it first on unproductive uses, such as prostitutes and drinking. Women, however, will figure out a way to use the funds to better the conditions of their families and often the community at large. Sometimes they start schools or small businesses that then allow their daughters to seek education instead of being shunted to low-paid work right away or being sold off in an arranged marriage.[6]

The promising microlending organization Kiva, for example, was founded by a woman and its clients are 80 percent female.[7] Similar results are beginning to be found in the economics literature (Kote and Honnakeri 2012). Measuring the success of these efforts for the individual small entrepreneur in developing countries is understandably quite difficult. There continues to be strong optimism that they reduce poverty for some people, although it is acknowledged that usually such lending agencies require ongoing financial support; so far the institutions required to make them self-financing have not been developed (Annim 2012).

Microfinance is interesting for another reason. It is one of the few poverty alleviation ideas that spread from the developing world to the developed world. Unfortunately, for several reasons microfinance has had difficulty helping the disadvantaged in the United States. While self-employment is a viable option for many poor people in the developing world, generally it is not in the United States. You cannot just sell tamales on the street corner or take care of children in your home without getting a significant number of licenses and permits and a tax number. You have to compete with large businesses that have advantages in negotiating with suppliers for lower costs or have national marketing campaigns. Some estimates are that only 8–20 percent of poor U.S. households would find self-employment a "viable livelihood strategy" (Schreiner and Morduch 2002, 23). For most poor people, self employment is a part of an income patching strategy, which may include some social safety net income. (Recall Lisa Servon's story about the woman named Lorraine from chapter 2.) A second reason concerns loan repayment. The Grameen Bank uses a joint-liability model, where the recipient of a loan is a member of a specific group and all members have a stake in seeing that a given loan is repaid. People in the United States, on the other hand, are very mobile, sometimes moving more than once a year, making the joint-liability model difficult to maintain.

To summarize, market institutions are the best, most sustainable, foundation for the virtuous cycle of prosperity and innovation that we will argue in chapter 25 is the foundation of a tempered and humane economy. There is nothing historically determined about prosperity. Every country will always have groups trying to hog its wealth through extractive institutions. Humane economies with pluralistic democracies do the best job of resisting the formation of extractive institutions in part because they have an active and thriving media to keep people informed and allow for the exchange of ideas.[8]

The focus of the chapter so far has been on the process of economic development. But it must be acknowledged that the economic development of some countries often has profound consequences for other countries which are already well developed. We could cite many examples, but perhaps the easiest way to understand the essential dynamics is to think about Japan and Germany. The data presented in Table 18.1 in the previous chapter shows that these are among the most prosperous large-population countries in the world. This is an achievement of the second half the twentieth century.[9] The productive capacity of these countries coming out of WWII was extremely compromised. They were effectively starting the development process from scratch.

Acemoglu and Robinson would point out that they both were quite effective in creating inclusive institutions—an important achievement in its own right. But we would argue there is more to the story. Both countries essentially pursued what economists call an export-led growth strategy. The basic idea of export-led growth is that in the process of developing the ability to export to already established markets industries will modernize, adopt new technologies, learn to market to sophisticated consumers, and generally develop an ability to compete in world markets. This process has lots of advantages to a country pursuing it—workers become better educated in order use the new technologies. The knowledge gradually spills over to other non-export sectors of the economy as workers change jobs.

This might seem like a win-win proposition for both the exporting countries and the United States because, make no mistake, they certainly exported to us. They got the development and we got the great cars and electronics and many other products. There were winners and losers because there always are, but benefits have exceeded costs. That's the creative destruction Acemoglu and Robinson mentioned. The problem is that both Germany and Japan made it a matter of national policy to export more than they import. That's a problem in a couple of different ways. The fact that it short-changes consumers in Germany and Japan is perhaps a matter best left to those countries to worry about.

But there are several effects on us that are our concern. The first is that there are industries in the United States that would be able to export to those countries if trade were balanced. Since it is not, U.S. employment and income are affected. Alfred Eckes Jr. (2011) has an excellent and nuanced history of the global economy highlighting the potentially negative effects of globalization. It is not easy to design programs to help those damaged by globalization because it is difficult in practice to separate the effects of globalization from the effects of technology. Putting these ideas together, some economists have suggested that the gains from trade could be used to help pay for programs, such as job retraining, that benefit large numbers of middle and lower income persons who are more likely to be negatively affected by globalization than people in the upper parts of the income distribution. (Recall we discussed who pays for job retraining from the behavioral economics angle in chapter 3.)

More systemic is the fact that running a surplus in the trade balance requires running a deficit in the capital account. In layperson's terms, large flows of financial capital came into the United States. Japan in particular is currently the second largest foreign holder of U.S. government debt. Large capital inflows have an effect on interest rates, keeping them lower than they would otherwise be. There are also exchange rate considerations that we needn't go into here (Highfill and Wojcikewych 2011).

It probably will not have escaped your notice that Germany and Japan are hardly the only countries to have used export-led growth. China's recent growth comes largely from export-led industries. They are now the largest foreign holder of U.S. government debt and their massive purchases of dollar denominated financial assets contributed greatly to the 2008 financial crisis. While this strategy made good sense for China, and they certainly have the right to improve the standard of living of their citizens, there was world-wide fallout from it. As a last note, while Germany and Japan developed inclusive institutions, China has yet to do so on the political side, and to some degree on the economic side. For that reason Acemoglu and Robinson forthrightly predict that the period of time that China will grow and develop is limited unless they reform their political institutions, making them more democratic (Acemoglu and Robinson 2012, 442).

Globalization, defined roughly as extending the rules and practices of markets beyond a country's borders, has basically made the world more prosperous. Countries learn from each other and trade with each other. In practical terms you're no longer just competing with people and firms in your own country, but around the world. It is more difficult for companies to establish national monopolies like those of the robber barons, so it is a kind of anti-trust program. But it has also increased income inequality. Jannett and some co-authors did a metadata analysis of foreign direct investment, finding that result (Clark et al. 2011). Ultimately the test of globalization may be the extent to which it fosters the strengthening of inclusive institutions around the world.

To live in a country not completely dominated by extractive institutions is a blessing. To live in one that aspires to inclusive institutions is better yet.

NOTES

1. Russia experienced rapid economic growth after WWII and China is doing so now. Russia was neither a market economy nor a democracy. China is not a democracy now, and either not or marginally a market economy.

2. Peacekeeping, on the other hand, is quite different. International peacekeeping forces have been relatively successful at such things as implementing peace agreements, enforcing power-sharing, supporting the rule of law and elections (Pinker 2012, 314–15).

3. He continues, "Overpopulation is overrated as a cause of starvation. Usually the worst problems occur in rural areas, not in cities" (Cowen 2012, 150).

4. To the extent that subsidies create surplus crops, when they are shipped abroad and sold at prices that are lower than they would be in the absence of the subsidies, local farmers in the destination countries are disadvantaged. Consumers in those destination countries benefit however.

5. Please see Muhammad Yunus (2007, with Karl Weber) *Creating a World Without Poverty: Social Business and the Future of Capitalism.*

6. Sanchez goes on to say: "As such, microlending undercuts traditional patriarchy. Interestingly, it does so in ways men tend to welcome. According to microlending advocates, men then tend to value the benefits a new business or job brings to family life, the extra income. They change their behavior and often their attitudes as a result. This is how societies progress."

7. See the Heifer International publication *World Ark*, the Holiday 2012 issue.

8. It does not follow that a little democracy is better than none. Semi-democracies, "anocracies," suffer from the worst of extractive institutions and do worse at insuring law and order than autocracies. Steven Pinker (2012, 310) quoting the *Global Report on Conflict, Governance, and State Fragility* "anocracies are 'about six times more likely than democracies and

two and one-half times as likely as autocracies to experience new outbreaks of societal wars' such as ethnic civil wars, revolutionary wars, and coups d'état."

9. Some scholars have even argued that by 1964 the economic growth of the "active belligerent losers" of World War II exceeded that of the "active belligerent winners" (Organski and Kugler 1977, 1363).

Chapter Twenty

When Markets Produce

Have you ever heard of the old "missionary barrels" where church ladies would collect clothes, put them in barrels, and send them to poor children on the western frontier? The children hated those clothes, free or not. You can just see the problem: a twelve-year-old farm girl ends up wearing a garment meant for a forty-year-old lady who hasn't been out of the city in her life. Now churches are more apt to have a "Church Mouse" resale shop—and selling the donations is better than giving them away. Making people pay for what they get, even if it is only 50 cents or a dollar, prompts them to be much more selective about what they take, and they are much happier with the items. They are also more apt to leave things they don't want so the next person has a chance at them.

Even when we are explicitly being charitable, markets are a powerful tool for achieving efficiency—in this case getting the donated clothing to the person who would enjoy wearing it the most. In chapter 18 we presented evidence that virtually all rich economies rely substantially on markets and in chapter 19 we argued that inclusive institutions are vital for creating and sustaining prosperity—precisely because they support markets. But markets create prosperity only under certain conditions, which economists summarize as free entry and exit, endowments that are not too unequal, and the effective operation of the price mechanism.[1]

We'll begin by thinking about an operational price mechanism because without it reward would not be related to contribution; that is, without a functional price mechanism the market principle would not hold. Visualize standing in a store aisle picking out a medicine for your allergies where there are choices two or three feet on either side of you for at least two or three shelves. With that rich of a choice set for consumers, the business behind the one you pick must be doing a lot of things right, producing a good product with the features you want and controlling costs; it must have a well-functioning supply and distribution chain. The employees of the successful company must work hard and smart to make and market a product that people want. In the long run businesses use the revenue generated from selling the product to reward—pay—their employees. Reward follows contribution, the basic market principle.

Economists like to say that "price" is a signal wrapped in an incentive. Customers signal to firms how much they value a particular item by how much they are willing to pay for it. In our example, the value of a particular medication is something only households can know. It takes time and experimentation to figure out how a given pill affects you—you need to do that yourself. The more people are willing to pay for a good or service the more likely it is that some firm will produce and sell it. Firms also use prices to give signals to customers. While pricing decisions are complex, the bottom line is that a firm will not stay in business in the long run if the price isn't high enough to pay its costs and make a profit, one side of market discipline. If producing one pill is much more costly than another, then the first one will only be produced if people are willing to pay a much higher price for it. So prices are a signal to firms about what people want, and a signal to customers about what the underlying costs of various products are.

To see how this works, suppose you're suffering from your allergies this morning. If a particular pill is 30 cents, it might be the best overall strategy for dealing with the health situation. If the pill is thirty thousand dollars, it is likely that you would figure out some other strategy, assuming allergies are an annoyance rather than a life threatening condition. At the thirty thousand dollar price tag, you would stay indoors during allergy season and make sure your HVAC has the best filtering system you can afford. Some medical products company would probably develop a mask to wear when jogging, or all the kids' soccer games would be played in an indoor air conditioned stadium. You get the idea; you'd make adjustments, and you should. One of the primary reasons markets create prosperity is that prices give good signals about the relative cost of things, whether it is efficient to use society's resources to alleviate allergies by a pill or by air conditioning. The economy is operating efficiently when the right medication (or air conditioning, etc.) is getting to the right people, at a price that reflects both how well the good or service works—its contribution to people's quality of life—and the cost to society of producing the good or service.

This argument assumes that the government has created the institutions that support markets. For example, that it has created "a level playing field" where all firms compete on an equal basis, and set some rules—for example, that the box actually contains what the label says it does, and that some safety regulations have been followed. In the language of chapter 19, the role of the government is to create inclusive institutions that allow firms free entry into the market—and then the government should let the markets work. Equally customers need to be free to enter or exit, to buy or not buy.

Another way to think about the importance of the price mechanism is to think about those occasions when it isn't allowed to work. Imagine that allergy medicine you like is suddenly available only by prescription. Is it still the right product for you? In a larger sense the question is the same, whether it is efficient for society to alleviate your suffering by the pill or by some other means. But the process of figuring that out is complicated for prescription medications when they are paid for by health insurance or some other third party. How do you make good decisions if you don't know what the price is? Do you count the cost of the doctor's visit to get the prescription? If you have an insurance copay, it is almost surely the case that the medication costs more than the copay, and to say that insurance pays the difference is only to say that all policy holders collectively are paying it. What health insurance does is introduce confusion about what the social cost of the pill really is. Even though you know there's more to it than that, when you're standing in a store aisle suffering you probably make your decision based just on the copay rather than mentally calculate its real cost.

The usefulness of prices as signals might well apply to medical interventions considerably more expensive than allergy medication. In our current system it is not easy for an individual to find out what a medical procedure usually costs (assuming things go well) before the procedure. The medical industry as a whole knows, for example, that if you have a particular procedure the total costs on average will be $3,000, but it's like pulling teeth to get them to tell you. We say the medical industry, because the well-meaning office staff person you get a callback from may well not know, nor have any easy way to find out. But the system knows because in the end each care provider gets paid for each procedure and any spreadsheet can be used to aggregate the data and calculate the average.

There is no obvious reason why some medical procedures couldn't be paid for pretty much the way as we do home renovations, for example, or car repairs. As far as the money aspects go, getting a colonoscopy could be about the same as getting a new patio door, or a hip replacement about the same as a kitchen renovation. Glasses, hearing aids, and root canals are already market transactions for many people because insurance doesn't cover them and they can run into thousands or tens of thousands of dollars in a short number of years. If you're immediately thinking about those people who couldn't save enough under any circumstances to afford a patio door or a kitchen renovation, then those people need help from the social safety net—in both housing and health expenditures.[2] When the resource endowments of some people are significantly below society's average then in general markets do not provide good outcomes for all persons.

But here we want to emphasize that when institutions are inclusive and the market-facilitating conditions are met, we favor market solutions—even for politically sensitive sectors like healthcare or the environment.[3]

When any one of the market conditions is not met, markets fail. Think about what economists call entry and exit, for example, whether or not you have real viable choices. Imagine you're carrying a heavy basket of laundry and miss the last step or two going down stairs. Unfortunately there's every chance you've broken a bone in your wrist or ankle. You call 911 and end up in the emergency room. There nothing analogous in this situation to standing in the store aisle trying to make a good decision about allergy medication. You need your bone set, surgery, a cast or whatever is required, whether the cost is a month's salary or a year's.

Everyone should have health insurance for emergencies. That is, markets handle this situation perfectly well as long as everyone is forward thinking enough to buy health insurance—assuming of course that there are enough different providers of private health insurance to provide a genuine choice. But endowments and prices are critical. You should certainly have bought health insurance if the price were about the same as your cell phone bill or your entertainment budget. What if it was as much as your rent or house payment? What if it was as much as your housing plus food plus transportation? For everyone there comes a point when the insurance company has effectively denied you coverage by making the premium too large a proportion of your income. In one way these people are in the same situation as the ones who couldn't afford a more routine health intervention. But surely the fact that they are facing a health emergency does matter.

Not only can the person in the health situation not walk away on a broken leg, no one can walk away from the chance that they might run into a similar health difficulty themselves. More importantly, we would argue that most people would not choose to walk away from doing their part to help people in distress—even if they had an iron-clad guarantee that they'd never need emergency room services themselves. Think about all the help volunteered in any kind of weather crisis. We do not believe anyone would seriously propose that people without health insurance should be sent home from an emergency room with a broken bone. How much to charge a patient without health insurance is a most difficult question. Chapter 23 is devoted to the economics of healthcare financing. But first in chapter 21 we make one more argument for markets, and in chapter 22 we think about the role of the government in tempering market outcomes and mitigating market failures in a more general way.

NOTES

1. Complete markets are also required.

2. This is an example of why complete markets are needed for an optimally functioning market economy in that we need to be able to insure against all future possible states of nature. Well functioning financial markets are way to make markets more complete because they facilitate saving against future eventualities; health insurance plays a similar role.

3. For one example, we briefly discuss the Nature Conservancy in chapter 22 when talking about the environment.

Chapter Twenty-One

Markets and Meaningful Work

Jannett has friends who love truck gardening; they love picking out the seeds, arranging the plants to cope with shade and soil interactions, managing moisture, and creating windbreaks. They produce more than they need themselves—Melinda takes produce everywhere she goes, to the beauty shop and Sunday school. At some point they began to think about a wider distribution, but giving tomatoes away to relative strangers runs into the same difficulty we talked about regarding the missionary barrel in the last chapter, how to get the vegetables to people who want them. So they took a flyer with getting a stand at a farmers market.

Gardening has now become a business for them. Yes, they need to deal with accountants and taxes. But more importantly they need to start thinking of their vegetables from the customer's point of view. People that shop at a farmers market have all the stands to compare, and they tend to be repeat customers. Either by talking to friends or by observation the gardeners quickly figured out that customers need to feel that they are getting good value for their money. The traditional language economists use is that there needs to be a "gain from trade" for both parties. The prices for the lettuce and tomatoes and pumpkins by season have to be set so that it is worthwhile for the gardener and the customer alike. In more general terms, you may recall we cited the idea from Steven Pinker in chapter 4 that markets help create empathy. Melinda and Jeff now spend considerable time trying to see their display, including prices, from the point of view of strangers browsing the market on a Saturday morning.

It's the repeat customers that keep a business going—and that may well prompt a great deal of ingenuity and creativity on the part of the business to keep them happy, make them feel they are getting a great value for their money. Markets are perfectly consistent with doing meaningful work. To say the same thing in negative terms, markets do not necessarily create a "dog-eat-dog" world of sharp or shady practices and confidence games. The market efficiency arguments in the last chapter actually require an institutional structure that punishes such behavior. That's easier said than done, as the tough love section and discussion of extractive institutions showed, but it's possible.

The important point for this chapter is that a person might choose to make their living in the market sector because they believe that doing so will facilitate their most meaningful work. Jannett's friends might choose to make their living from truck gardening, even if they quit their better paying jobs to do so and their income is permanently less than it would have been teaching school, or whatever the alternative was. Most people don't start businesses of their own; they work for others. But market efficiency still requires the same reasoning. Every business has to find things to sell at a price where there are gains for both sides: customers get good value for their money; the business makes a profit. Prices are the mechanism to achieve the gains from trade.

Large organizations are complex and they have to develop the internal structures to manage information well, especially the information embedded in prices and buyers' reactions to prices. Every employee makes decisions that affect customers directly or indirectly. Using buyer and price information is always difficult, but a large organization has to do it well enough to survive.

Large organizations are not necessarily businesses of course; some nonprofit organizations and governmental agencies resemble large businesses in many ways. The crucial difference concerns the way they get their money. The government gets its money from taxpayers, and the nonprofits from donations (to oversimplify considerably). There is a huge divide between the people receiving the services or products from the nonprofit or government agency and the people paying the bills. A business gets its money from customers; it's the same people receiving the good or service and paying the bills. A business serves one master so to speak; a non-business organization serves two. Both kinds of organizations have to solve the information problems involved with getting the right service to the right people, and there is no reason to suppose that businesses do a worse job with the information problems than other organizations of comparable size and complexity. Even ignoring the information and signaling problems, the nonprofit or government agency may in some cases have to prioritize satisfying the desires of whoever is paying the bills, even when that means shortchanging the people receiving the services—at least from the latter's point of view.

So suppose you are a person with a passion for improving the lives of others by getting them organic vegetables, for example. You could join (or start) either a nonprofit organization or a business to do this. To make the choice even more stark, suppose there is no reason in particular to think you'll make any more or less money in your paycheck going one way as compared to the other. If your motivation is to help people, you might well choose to go the market route, to avoid the problem of serving two masters.

One more observation. Creativity cannot be coerced and it is not self-evident that it can be purchased either. We're not going to open a can of worms about whether you can do things to make yourself more creative, let alone make others so. But you can set up the institutions in such a way that markets reward creativity, even understanding that, beyond achieving whatever they consider to be a regular life-style, money may not motivate the most creative minds in either the arts or the sciences. Meeting the challenge of markets can be perfectly consistent with meaningful work under the right conditions. The next section takes up some common areas where those conditions are not met.

V

Tempering Markets and Government Policy

Chapter Twenty-Two

The Government We Make

Good government is one of the most important ways we temper markets to create an economy which is sturdy and flexible rather than brittle and prone to failure. A *pure* market economy does not create widespread prosperity. Market failures are human failures, and behavioral economics has helped us structure our thinking about them. The government creates and maintains institutions to support strong markets, and it helps us deal with market failures. In a democracy the government is ultimately a tool of the electorate, with voting being the decision making mechanism as discussed in chapter 8. Jannett's mother has a saying, "You have the children you raise." By extension, we have the government we create.

In section II one of the key ideas is that we rely on the government for important parts of our education system and retirement planning. We referred to these institutions and arrangements by the traditional economist's term "social contract." The economist Robert Frank suggests the name "the libertarian welfare state" for these kinds of government programs (1985, 244 ff). Here we're going to introduce the term "self-imposed tough love." Both our term and Frank's seem contradictory at first. It takes some explaining, and we find it easier to begin with individuals and families.

We learned from behavioral economics that people respond to incentives in interesting ways. For example, we've heard of people who sign a contract to pay $100 to the political party they hate if they don't keep a certain commitment—say to stop smoking or to learn a foreign language. This is an example of what we mean by self-imposed tough love. Self-imposed, nobody can make you sign the contract, but tough love, there are tough consequences if you don't follow through. The essential feature of self-imposed tough love is that you make choices today that will constrain your future behavior. Behavioral economists call these things commitment devices.[1]

Living in a family as opposed to breaking up a family could be described as self-imposed tough love, self-discipline. At least for adults, you choose to form a family; you choose how much you are involved with your immediate family; you choose how broad your family network is, who "counts" as family. Most people realize that in making these choices they are putting constraints on their own behavior. This is out of concern and love for other family members, but it also helps us do things for our personal benefit that our life experience (not to mention behavioral economics) has taught us we'd be less likely to do on our own. Your family might be the reason you stick to a resolution to diet or follow your treatment plan for your diabetes.

The social contract relating education and Social Security can be thought of in a similar way. Remembering the insights from behavioral economics, most people put more emphasis on the present than is optimal, and they have difficulty evaluating risks over long periods of time. Especially in the past, some people did not see the value in education beyond the three R's, not realizing how different future production would be. Compulsory education is the tough love society has chosen for that. In addition, you know you should save for your retirement, but in the press of daily living you don't get that done. In those circumstances you might be glad for a program, Social Security for example, that you are required to pay into now but promises you benefits when you retire. The tough love part is making you prepare for retirement, something you know you should do. The self-imposed part comes from the fact we live in a democracy. While everyone can think of ways to improve public education or Social Security, we would bet few of us would vote to eliminate them altogether.

For another example of using the government for self-imposed tough love think of the labor movement we discussed in the Mother Jones chapter. Working conditions at the beginning of the unionization movement could not have been more risky for many workers. And while the labor movement was partly a response to employers, it was also a way to get workers to cooperate with each other, for example, to advocate legislation that enforces certain safety regulations that each might have forgone for a higher wage. The argument for a minimum wage is similar, it prevents workers from bidding the wage down to subsistence levels. Tough love—a given worker can't work for less than the stated rate. Self-imposed—you choose whether or not to work at that particular place. To be a bit careful in our argument, while some aspects of the labor environment are mandated by government (e.g., workplace safety), quite a bit of it comes from the possibility of unionization, rather than direct union pressure, because of the decline of unions in American society. If the work conditions in a given firm are too objectionable, the workers can form a union and negotiate for improvements. We use our government to create laws to allow for, and regulate, unionization.

To generalize from these important examples, on the societal level "self-imposed tough love" refers to situations where the government helps us (1) deal with widespread risk over many years, and (2) make choices in the present that will constrain future behavior. You may recall we had an entire section on "tough love" by itself—the kind imposed by others rather than self-imposed. Our primary focus there was on the implications of imposing the market principle on the poor but not the rich, and we concluded that to do so would be hypocritical and unfair. Here we are arguing that forming and maintaining the institutions required for strong markets is one important type of self-imposed tough love.

Our next example of self-imposed tough love concerns the environment. We have made substantial progress in environmentalism and green economics, but we still have important work to do.

Jannett comes from a family background that is agricultural.[2] In a way they are as connected to the canyons and creeks and cropland as they are to family members. Their commitment to the environment must be consistent with earning a living from the land—in the most serious sense environmentalism is their vocation, not an avocation. From one angle many of the decisions they make concerning the environment are similar to other business decisions. A farmer decides how close to the house to plow (that is, how much land is "lawn" instead of "cropland") in much the same way many of us decide how much time to spend checking email from work instead of asking the kids how their day went at school. In prosperous countries like ours, markets allow us to express our concern for the environment in the most practical of ways. If, for example, you believe that a particular piece of land should be taken out of cultivation and returned to wetlands, you can buy the property and do it. The Nature Conservancy, for example, is a privately funded organization we admire that does exactly that.

The major environmental-economic problem is when markets fail because the buyer or seller ignores some important cost or benefit of the transaction, what economists call externalities. If one person or business pollutes the land, a stream via runoff, or the air with emissions, she is not just making a decision that affects herself; it can affect many people. Clean air and water are vital to life on earth. Global warming may affect virtually everyone for decades into the future. Tough love in this case means requiring people to take responsibility for the externalities they create—and that can only be done in most cases by the government. The large economics literature on the effects of pollution reduction, cost containment, and the impact of environmental policies on economic growth suggests that this kind of government policy is fairly mature. By and large, as a society we have concluded that government policies may be required to reduce pollution or protect the environment.

The Clean Air Act of 1963, the Clean Water Act of 1972, and subsequent amendments to both have materially improved our environment. From 1970 to 2012 in the United States there has been a 70 percent decline in aggregate air emissions of the six most common pollutants (carbon monoxide, lead, nitrogen oxides, volatile organic compounds, particulate matter, and sulfur dioxide).[3] For water, from 1965 to 1997 there has been a decline in DDT and from 1975 to 1997 in lead contaminants.[4] On the other hand, carbon dioxide emissions went up by 30 percent over the same period and polyaromatic hydrocarbon water contamination increased between 1975 and 2000. The general conclusion is that the "low-hanging fruit" of reducing water and air pollution has been achieved. The large emitters (factories, mines, etc.) have already been addressed by the Clean Air and Clean Water Acts. Now we have to tackle the harder problem of making widespread but small-scale changes.

Global warming affects both air and water—but it is orders of magnitude more complicated. It's global, not local. The primary negative effects are decades into the future. Dealing with it requires immediate local expenditures to handle global damages felt mainly by the children of our children, but it's an economic problem and should be treated as such. Increasing prosperity brings us things that make life better: heat and air conditioning, air travel. Global warming would not be a problem if economic growth stopped. That needs emphasis. The global warming problem would essentially solve itself if we were willing to live with no economic growth. But as economists, that seems to be a dire solution—one that is unlikely to be acceptable to most people in the United States and the developed world, let alone countries in the developing world.

Strategies for coping will have to involve adaption, geoengineering, and mitigation—all of these. Adaption can be small scale and local. As sea levels rise, people will be forced over time to move to higher ground. Geoengineering will help, for example, through new technologies in energy production and transportation, or in heating, air conditioning, and insulation. Bjorn Lomborg (2007, 21) has interesting ideas about reducing global warming. Cities create "heat islands" because they are drier (rainwater and snowmelt are drained away on purpose) and because they have vast amounts of black asphalt and dark structures that absorb the sun's heat. Lomborg suggests more parks with trees, ponds, and fountains, and reroofing buildings and paving with lighter colors could decrease city temperatures dramatically, perhaps as much as five degrees in Los Angeles. Levitt and Dubner discuss some far out ideas (remember Buck Rogers?) such as the Super Sink, a device made from old tires, to reduce the intensity of hurricanes (2009, 160–63), or pumping sulfur dioxide into the stratosphere to reflect sunlight away from the earth (2009, 193–97).

This may be a good moment to remember that the politics of global warming very often get ahead of the science. We often have to make important decisions before we know as much as we'd like about their eventual outcomes. In the case of the environment, for example, we do not now know whether there are "tipping points" in the capacity of the atmosphere to absorb pollutants. Although not all global warming comes from greenhouse gasses, and methane and water vapor are arguably as important as carbon dioxide, it's the latter that gets the media attention and political traction—and so that is our focus. Carbon dioxide emissions are a side effect of everyday activities. The effects are both positive and negative, but the latter will dominate in the long run if nothing is done.

This is another example of externalities. It's a market failure; carbon emissions are costless for the emitter. The only realistic solution is to make them costly. We use economic jargon like the "carbon price," but essentially we need to create the institutions that require us to pay for our emissions. There are two strategies for doing that: one is a carbon tax and the other is a cap and trade system, like the one that was proposed in the now-lapsed Kyoto initiative. Economists strongly prefer either system to "command and control type regulations" on efficiency grounds, although neither is simple to design and administer. But Kyoto failed because it was also a top-down global initiative. It was nothing like self-imposed; many countries were not willing to have Kyoto policies imposed on them. On the other hand, many countries have developed their own local carbon emission markets which seem more promising (Newell, Pizer, and Raimi 2013). We have to say, however, that some economists have serious concerns about countries free riding on the efforts of others. William Nordhaus has even proposed that any country which does not join international efforts to tackle global warming be hit with significant tariffs on products exported anywhere in the world (2013, 8). That's strong medicine that would get any country's attention.

We also need to mention that there is considerable tension between global poverty alleviation and pollution reduction. The environmental problems of the developing world are so significant and complex we cannot even scratch the surface here. Over the next two or three decades, almost all the growth in energy demand—and the concomitant greenhouse gasses—will be in the developing world (Wolfram, Shelef, and Gertler 2012). The economists Catherine Wolfram, Orie Shelef, and Paul Gertler remind us that "keeping families in poverty is not a way to reduce energy demand" and we certainly agree (2012, 135).

Another important issue involves a third necessity for life, as important as air and water, although not in the news as often. That is fertile soil. Many a war has been fought over crop land, and many a migration triggered by the depletion of soil fertility. Deforestation in South America and Africa as farmers carve out land for crops to replace used-up fields has been a major cause of erosion and the silting up of surface water supplies. Solutions require the cooperation of many individual farmers—and considerable research into both farming technology and how to convince farmers to change long-standing practices. To mention just one of many possible examples, as reported by Mark Guarino in *The Christian Science Monitor* (October 25, 2013), the Howard G. Buffett Foundation is currently funding research to help small farmers in Africa with their conservation practices. Howard Buffett himself does no-till farming on his Illinois farm and believes that may be the best general solution to erosion problems and land fertility depletion, ideas being tested out on research farms in Arizona and South Africa.

In summary, green economics is a field that is growing in importance; its challenges are attracting a lot of good talent and ideas. As economic problems go, we're midway on this one. Progress made; work to do.

The last main topic in this chapter on the government is the social safety net. The problems here are not so much specific market failures as systemic failures. It sometimes seems as if the current mix of government programs making up the social safety net is disliked by everyone because the programs do not distinguish between bad decisions and bad luck. Some people object because they do not feel that the programs are sufficiently sensitive to life's misfortunes. Others hate it because they see bad decisions being rewarded and good decisions being ignored. Clearly this is a major social contract in need of rethinking. Along the lines of Amartya Sen, the political philosopher Ronald Dworkin has recently argued in *The New York Review of Books* (November 7, 2013) that any society, ours in particular, needs to achieve economic equality. "We achieve true economic equality . . . not when everyone has the same wealth, no matter what decisions he has made in the course of his life, but when what one has depends only on those decisions, and not on good or bad luck in health, accident, or inheritance."

The question is how such a goal could be politically attainable given the practical difficulties of the world in which we live. Dworkin proposes

> an economically sophisticated theory of taxation by way of answer: a redistributive tax system should be modeled on a hypothetical insurance scheme. The fortunate should pay, by way of taxes, what that model suggests they would have paid, by the way of premiums, in an actual insurance market; the unfortunate should receive, by way of social benefits, what they would have been entitled to receive in that insurance market.

This idea is quite similar to Robert Frank's idea of the libertarian welfare state. You may recall that one of his insights is that the rich will favor a progressive income tax at least in part because they realize status must be paid for.

In order to begin thinking about what such an insurance scheme would be like, consider the following simple example. Suppose two twenty-year-old men with exactly the same life circumstances have the same opportunity to get some education. If either one chooses to get the education then he is guaranteed to earn an income that is ten times what he could otherwise earn. Both men have the same opportunity, but the schooling is challenging and difficult. In our current system, if one man chooses to take the schooling and the other does not, then even if they work the same amount the one earning the higher income will pay much more in income and other taxes than the one who does not get the schooling. Under the insurance scheme, the person who chose to not get the education would not receive any social benefits to make up for the income differential because it was a choice, not luck, that made the difference. Of course we're immediately thinking that real life is complicated, and a realistic insurance plan would need to be more nuanced. But that is the idea. The person who chose to not get the education would not be rewarded by the taxing system for that choice, for example, he would not receive a benefit from an earned income tax credit type program.[5]

To change the thought experiment a bit, suppose that the same two men at age twenty have both chosen to get the schooling, but there is only one opening. Suppose that since they are equally qualified it's essentially a coin flip which man gets the education. In this case the man who wins the coin flip would pay more in income taxes than the other man. Not only that, remembering that the better job pays ten times what the other job pays, he would actually have to pay more than ten times the amount of income tax. In this example, the unlucky person might receive some benefits from an earned income tax credit type program. Again, there are many compounding factors in real life that would have to be taken into account, but economic research can help. Our assumption is that the two men were in the same situation when they were twenty years old. Since in real life no two people are ever exactly identical, we'd have to figure out what it would mean to be substantially identical, for the purposes of insurance. There is already a significant research program underway to study exactly that question, what it would mean to say that people have "equal opportunity" (Roemer 2012).

One of the most profound questions in regard to equal opportunity we've already talked about extensively in the education chapter—how to think about parents' activities in regard to giving their children a head start in the competition for things like educational opportunities. On the one hand, if I make the appropriate sacrifices, shouldn't I be able to put my child in the situation where his chance of getting the opportunity is say 60–40 percent rather than 50–50 percent? On the other hand, from a child's point of view, why should someone else get a better chance at the training just because her parents were in a different economic situation than mine were? These are profound questions to be decided by society at large—but once society makes its decision, then it's up to the economists to provide the appropriate strategies.

A policy change to implement an insurance-type social safety net would require not only the theory, but also the relevant data, and then the required political action. As for the data, think about what the IRS already knows or can find out from your financial advisor, and the information available from people's phones since they seem quite willing to use them to check into airline flights or as a payment device. It may well be that the crucial problem is not data availability but working out the privacy issues involved, which would be substantial.[6] We don't make any particular predictions about how the taxing system and social safety net will change over time, but we are confident they will, and with improvements in both theory and data, those changes could be improvements.

In this chapter we've focused on things that seem especially important as we look to the future: education/Social Security, labor market conditions, the environment, and an improved social safety net. Although incremental improvements are always necessary and important, reflect on the fact that society has achieved things that would have been considered pie-in-the-sky utopian dreams during the Great Depression.

The common thread of these programs is that they all involve significant attempts to mitigate risk over long periods of time. They all involve making good decisions now for benefits that accrue over many years. It's no accident that Dworkin called the improved social safety net a kind of insurance. In fact, we would argue that the government as a whole acts as a kind of "insurer of last resort." We're making an analogy to the federal government's role as a lender of last resort. When the economy teeters on the edge of a recession caused by problems in the financial markets, the government acts as a lender of last resort. Doing so is also acting as an insurer of last resort, and it is quite important that what is being insured is the health of the entire economy, not just the particular financial institutions. We'd argue something analogous for all of the programs we've talked about in this chapter. They are designed to help the entire economy deal with large scale systemic risk over substantial periods of time. They are designed to help the economy prosper in the face of such risks. For individuals you can think of buying insurance as self-imposed tough love, self-discipline. We're making the same argument for the government of a tempered and humane economy.

NOTES

1. There is an extensive economics literature on commitment devices. See, for example, Beshears et al. (2011).
2. Jannett also has a scholarly interest in municipal recycling: Highfill and McAsey (1997).
3. "Air Quality Trends." September 3, 2013, EPA.

4. Larsen Matthew C., Pixie A. Hamilton, and William H. Werkheiser. 2013. "Water Quality Status and Trends in the United States," *Monitoring Water Quality*. Elsevier: 33–34.

5. To be a bit careful, we are not arguing that either man made a good or bad decision. It is often wise to sacrifice income in service of other important goals. But if you choose to do that, then the taxing system shouldn't implicitly be based on the idea that you had no choice in the matter.

6. On the political front, the rich might decide they ultimately approve of society creating a tough love type system where each individual grandchild has to live with the consequences of his or her decisions. It is tough to say no to your own grandchild even when you know you should; sometimes it's easier to have the government play the heavy. A similar argument might have some traction with all income groups, because the other side of controlling for luck is that individuals can no longer use "bad luck" as a cover for "bad decisions." In some ways, that is the most basic meaning of tough love. It would benefit both the individuals and society in that it would send clearer signals to individuals about the consequences of decisions. Although behavioral economics suggests that reacting to signals isn't easy in the short run, in the long run economic prosperity is impossible without it.

Chapter Twenty-Three

When the Challenge Is Healthcare

For each of us healthcare is ultimately a matter of life and death, so we are devoting a separate chapter to the economics of healthcare. Some aspects we've already talked about, buying allergy pills at the drugstore, for example. But health and sickness are central to the human condition in ways that are far more significant than we have so far acknowledged. We have argued that there is a moral foundation to the economy, affecting both individuals and society at large as expressed by our government, and in this chapter we will argue that there are some significant moral hazards affecting our healthcare and healthcare financing.

Steven Brill, a reporter for *TIME* magazine (March 4, 2013), investigating healthcare finance, tells the story of a woman Alice D., her husband Steven D.'s illness and death, and the aftermath. In his final interview with her she said "I'm never going to remarry. I can't risk the liability." There had been considerable family tension about which medical interventions to have. Steven D. wanted every possible treatment to prolong his life. Alice D. said "Steven kept saying he wanted every last minute he could get, no matter what. But I had to be thinking about the cost and how all this debt would leave me and my daughter." He died eleven months after receiving the diagnosis; his treatment cost $902,452. After all the adjustments and insurance payouts, Alice D. still owed $142,000 she didn't have. The bill collectors were calling and writing letters. It's almost impossible to wrap your head around such difficult circumstances, but the financial consequences of health situations can often be dire. Medical expenses are a leading cause of bankruptcy in the United States even for some people who have health insurance as Steven D. had.

It's a complicated subject, with issues concerning both healthcare providers and the recipients of healthcare. Healthcare involves risks, the effects sometimes accumulating over many years. We'll start with the moral hazard of providers. Unfortunately, the effectiveness of medical tests and procedures in improving the patient's health outcome is all too often quite uncertain. Those tests and procedures can be time consuming, cause discomfort, and be expensive. Just because a procedure is common does not ensure that later it will not be scientifically shown to be no more effective than a placebo. This was the case for a surgery to deal with chest pain, and another for knee pain, the latter done often enough that more than $1 billion has been spent on it (Ariely 2008, 174–75). It's often a tough call for a doctor to make, weighing the patient's discomfort and hopes against the chance that the procedure does not improve the outcome for the patient. It seems bizarre that the doctor's own income should be affected in any way by the decision made, but often it is. And it defies the laws of human nature to suppose that fact never affects, consciously or otherwise, the decision made.

To rely on markets to correct this situation would require that patients have good and timely price information, something which, to put it politely, cannot be taken for granted. More importantly, it would require that patients be able to "walk away" if the price seemed to them to be excessive given the probable outcome of the procedure or test. When that isn't possible, then a market solution cannot even be imagined. Questioning a doctor's recommendations may even be a ticket to being dismissed from the practice, and changing doctors or clinics in the middle of an extensive and serious health treatment is something most of us would prefer to avoid. This is a market failure precisely because market forces will not normally solve it. Compensation plans, however, could perfectly well be changed so that no healthcare provider's income depends on whether a particular test is done or treatment plan followed. At the Mayo Clinics, for example, doctors' compensation is related to the number of patients they see, but not to the tests they order. The trend toward far fewer single doctor practices might facilitate similar policies elsewhere.

We argued in a previous chapter that some procedures, even expensive ones, might be well handled by the market. The key issue is whether or not the patient can walk away. We used the example of a broken leg for when you can't walk away, and we argued that private health insurance is a good way to go, as long as when you buy the insurance you have genuine choices. But unfortunately, insurance poses a moral hazard of its own on the buyer side of the market. So let's think about how health insurance works for a moment. Any viable insurance scheme has to set the rates so that the amount paid in each year is enough to pay the group's medical expenses and have something left over for administration (which in the United States is not inexpensive).

People who have better than average health will pay in more premiums than their own medical expenses; for people with worse than average health their medical bills are larger than their premiums. If health were completely random, with everyone having about the same health risks as everyone else, then health insurance would be roughly equivalent to the insurance for many other things such as a house, car, and so on. But typically the younger you are, the healthier you are. (We strongly hope this is the case, although we are certainly aware of situations where it is not.) The moral hazard in this case is that people might decide to not buy health insurance until they reach an age where they are more likely to run into significant health concerns. The social contract has to be such that young healthy people have to buy insurance many years before they are likely to need it themselves. For historical reasons that don't need to detain us, in the United States this deal was and is essentially enforced by employers. Employers offer health insurance, and it is mandatory for all employees, young and old alike, healthy or not. Increasingly, this system has come under stress. The first great source of this stress was people living much longer after retirement. Employer provided health insurance proved inadequate to take care of the elderly, so Medicare was introduced.

In our current system the majority of people who do not have health insurance are the working poor—whose employers do not provide health insurance. In 2012, 15.4 percent of Americans did not have health insurance; 12.9 percent of children in poverty did not have health insurance.[1] Part time employees, many of them being the income patchers we mentioned in chapter 2, are especially hard hit with 27.7 percent being without health insurance. Sarah Kliff of the *Washington Post* reported in October of 2011 that Walmart would no longer be providing health insurance to new part-time employees, although it had done so since 1996. Medicaid does help, with actually more Americans covered by Medicaid than Medicare. The Affordable Care Act may change these dynamics, although it will be a while before any data is available.

In the future there will be another stress on the current system felt by persons of all incomes. Increasingly even middle class families will not have employer provided health insurance. Partly that is because employers believe that employees don't value health insurance as much as they value a commensurate increase in pay; employers also do not want to bear the increasing risk associated with the rising cost of healthcare. An economist for whom we have the highest respect informally argues that all corporations, including Fortune 500 ones, will stop offering health insurance to employees within the next ten years—it will no longer be one of those employee benefits that the middle and upper middle classes can count on. We're not sure about that, but it seems like a real possibility.

No matter what exact changes are coming we have to create health insurance schemes that are financially viable. In plain English that requires a system where the healthy are required to pay for the health expenditures of the sick. From one angle people might understand that paying for other people's expenses when they are healthy is absolutely required if they are to have any reason to hope that healthy people will pay for their expenses when they are sick. But the temptation will still be to game the system, wait to buy insurance when healthy, buy it only when sick. The solution will certainly involve the government in some way—because only the government can require large-scale non-voluntary actions. Just like the government requires all drivers to have car insurance, the only solution is to require every young and healthy person to have health insurance and that is one purpose of the Affordable Care Act. Mandatory insurance is always a kind of self-imposed tough love. The devil is in the details, of course, but the general trend is inescapable.[2] Douglas Hough (2013), taking a behavioral economics point of view, recommends many small well-designed fixes for our large problems with healthcare—believing those might accumulate into a better system.

The temptation for the healthy to wait to buy health insurance or for doctors to let their own incomes influence their care decisions are not the only market failures related to healthcare. Sometimes there are externalities, not dissimilar from the environmental ones discussed in the previous chapter. The benefits to containing a flu epidemic go far beyond the individual's benefit of getting a flu shot—it may certainly be in society's best interest to subsidize flu shots for vulnerable populations. Preventing the spread of illness is the motivation for the series of shots required for children to attend public schools in most states. As long as society has any role in paying for the healthcare of older Americans, that is, as long as we have Medicare or anything like it, it may prove to be an economically sound policy to pay for preventive health maintenance for that end of the age spectrum as well. Because such a large part of the costs of healthcare involve chronic conditions, it saves money in the long run to begin treating those conditions earlier in life. For this reason Steven Brill, the reporter for *TIME* magazine we mentioned before, argues that lowering the age of Medicare a couple of years would actually save money. For that matter, because of the advances in medical records and coding, it would probably be possible to design a system where persons with certain chronic conditions are automatically enrolled in Medicare regardless of age.

Another problem is the perverse pricing strategy sometimes found for medical items and procedures. Hospitals, for example, often have high list prices. Brill reports that most insurance plans and Medicare negotiate a lower price, so that hospitals only realize about 35 percent on average of the list prices. We've heard people say that these high list prices are a way to "price discriminate," by charging rich people without insurance high prices so that hospitals can afford to treat indigent. The problem with that is that rich Americans almost always have insurance, and in most hospitals there are not enough rich uninsured foreigners to make any difference. Thus it is that slice of people either without insurance, or whose insurance is not very good, who actually pay the list price. As with compensation schemes, this is a problem which is solvable. For example, suppose the government passed a law saying that any price which is charged to anyone for an essential component of a normal healthcare procedure must be offered to everyone. (Medicare standards could be used to define normal and essential.) The hospitals would then set its prices to achieve the same level of revenue for a given set of circumstances. Everyone would pay the same for essentials; the very prosperous would pay more, but only for amenities.

A more difficult problem is at the intersection of high list prices, third party payer systems, and medical uncertainty. We made an argument in chapter 20 that even expensive healthcare items should be paid for directly (just like buying a patio door) if they are not an emergency and there are no externalities involved. But in the uncertain world of medicine, knowing what is an emergency is not always easy. There may be a continuum between plenty of time to plan and things that need immediate attention. The problem arises for situations in the middle of this continuum when the costs or prices are quite high. David Colander tells a story of a seventy-year-old man who unfortunately was not recovering from surgery as quickly as expected (Colander 2013, 110). He wasn't regaining weight and had to spend weeks in the hospital with a bill to Medicare of nearly $275,000. The medical staff eventually figured out that his dentures were the problem. Fixing them cost $75, which was not covered by Medicare—and the man refused the treatment. This kind of story is not uncommon. It may be that the man has trouble dealing with the size of the numbers. Perhaps $75 feels real but a big number like $275,000 is too abstract—it just seems like Monopoly money. It may be that the person is pretty selfish, and these two answers are not mutually exclusive.

Decisions in healthcare, both in financing and in the choice of medicines and procedures, are subject to all the insights from behavioral economics we thought about in chapters 3, 5, and 6. Patients react to the way choices are framed, and physicians are often loss-averse; examples can be found in Hough (2013). Coming up with strategies to deal with this problem will be a continuing challenge, one that is essentially the same whether a person has public or private insurance. This may be a place for increased research by behavioral economists in collaboration with healthcare professionals. Ariely (2008, 62–63, 121) has suggested that behavioral economics can help with the common problem of procrastination—either make widely avoided procedures free, or bundle them so that many can be done at the same time based on easily remembered milestones—age, or time from the last checkup like car maintenance.

There is one more market-related issue we need to think about. A friend of Pat's who recently took a child to a Mayo Clinic remarked "The doctors actually talked to each other." What he meant was that the child was being treated as a whole human being, not just eyes in one folder, circulation in another, and weight loss in a third. The care was coordinated—not to mention that there is a lot of knowledge in a room with three or four doctors who talk to each other. So we need specialists, but even more we need for their efforts to be coordinated—something that currently falls through the cracks in many places. One way to achieve that would be to subsidize an increase in family practitioners, and that's where the market failure comes in. When there are barriers to entry a shortage of doctors will occur, and inevitably the fields with the highest pay and prestige will fill first, leaving unfilled positions at the bottom of the pay and prestige hierarchy. Why family practitioners are on the bottom is itself a vital question, but in any event, eliminating barriers to entry in medical schools and licensing would increase their number.[3]

One of the blessings of living in the current day is the availability of medical technologies that improve lives, technologies that were not available a generation ago and were not even dreamed of two generations ago. In our own families we have been blessed by these technologies, and we would be surprised if your family has been completely untouched by similar health situations. The problem is a level of cost beyond any of the examples we've talked about so far. A treatment might be two or three times the household annual income, and the family member might need it every year for the rest of his or her life. In some situations the cost could be a multiple of the household lifetime income.

The key issue here is again the structure of health insurance, although moral hazard is not involved. We need to think about health insurance from a completely different angle. Think about house insurance as an analogy. Most families would find the loss of their house in a fire to be difficult to recover from, but the risk is rather small; therefore insurance companies can sell a policy at a reasonable cost that essentially spreads the cost of the loss from a house fire across many households. But insurance companies have to plan carefully for events like the 2013 meteor strike in Russia. If everyone's house burns down then the insurance scheme fails. If, for example, the insurance company were to try to build a reserve large enough to pay for everyone's house burning down within a twenty-year window, then effectively your annual premium would have to exceed one twentieth of the value of your house. The implication is that insurance only works for unlikely events.

But the technological improvements in healthcare, while a great blessing, increase the likelihood that every family will experience a health situation with much larger economic consequences than a house fire. In the past, in a heart-breaking way, it was simpler for a family which had a significant health crisis. Before the technology was available, there was nothing to be decided.

Now that excellent but expensive technologies are so much more available, someone has to decide what to do.

In our current system the family has to make impossible decisions if the technology is not covered by their insurance—and we have just argued that insurance cannot cover expensive technologies for a great many people. Sometimes the sick person has to decide whether to risk the impoverishment of everyone they love for a modest gain in their own chance of survival or improvement in their quality of life. It goes without saying they wouldn't risk impoverishing their family under normal circumstances, but facing death? They very well may have worked hard their whole life to support this family. No one in extremis should be expected to place a dollar value on a possibly life-saving intervention, nor should their family members have to do so—that's just not humane.

Imagine the person who is wisest in your family as a guide in helping you think through these things. There are medical interventions currently available that would cost enough to affect the prosperity of your family forever, with a negative effect on both the quality of life and life expectancy of every family member. Some night you might dimly see out of the corner of your eye that in a moment of desperation and panic you might make a decision to sacrifice the future of some family members in order to be able to afford a given medical intervention.

Once you have crossed that Rubicon, with your family wisdom and the help of your spiritual advisor you might be willing to sign a release so that when the day comes that your health is on the line, no one even tells you about the expensive treatment that the insurance only partially covers, so that to get it would impoverish your family. Living wills are meant to relieve some of the stress of these decisions, but this is about having the decision never come up. We have argued forcefully that having choices is valuable, but in this instance it may be that we would prefer a system where neither the individual nor family has to choose. End of life decisions break hearts, break up families, prolong grief by decades. We have some friends, married for many years, who both have significant health concerns. They have found doctors they trust and have the medical interventions their insurance covers. They don't even talk with their doctors about anything not covered. That is their family wisdom.

Living in a country where we don't force anyone to make these heart breaking choices might strengthen families. Over the course of this book we have thought long and hard about the ways the wisdom of families can improve the economy. Now, in the case of healthcare, it is possible that we could structure the healthcare system in a way that strengthens families.

NOTES

1. For persons without health insurance and income patchers without health insurance: U.S. Census Bureau, Current Population Reports, Income, Poverty and Health Insurance Coverage in the United States: 2012. Table 7.

For children in poverty without health insurance: U.S. Census Bureau, Current Population Reports, Income, Poverty and Health Insurance Coverage in the United States: 2012. Figure 11.

2. Modern rich countries have developed many different institutional systems for health-care provision and financing. We have to find a path up the mountain, but it probably is worth remembering that according to Taylor "no country seems fully happy with its health care system" (2012, 109).

3. There seems to be some debate about whether the essential barrier to entry is the lack of slots in medical schools, the lack of slots in residency programs, or our inability or unwillingness to use international talent. We suspect all three of these play a role.

VI

Looking to the Future

Chapter Twenty-Four

The Wisdom of Families—Challenge and Aspiration

The previous sections have focused primarily on the present—sometimes looking at the past to see how we arrived at this point, sometimes trying to follow a thread from the past a short way into the future. But basically we were in the here and now. In this section we want to look toward the future. In order to present our ideas as simply as possible, in the next chapter we present flow-chart models of the economy: first of the market principle in action, second of the family principle in action, and finally of a tempered and humane economy that encompasses both. Much of what we say will not be particularly controversial—although some of it might be. Economists often disagree, but up to this point in the book all the economics literature we have cited, whether theory or statistics, has been mainstream. Some of what we will say next is equally well established. But in some ways our ideas are ahead of the literature—you could even say we hope these ideas will be a major research agenda for the discipline of economics. Our essential vision is of measured optimism. People, young people especially, who feel empowered at home, will expect to be contributors, not free-riders, in the larger society. That's a reason for optimism.

But we don't want to imply that day to day life will be utopian. Alain de Botton and John Armstrong make an argument that resonates with us, that we often have difficulty judging the historical significance of our own time. "The things that are happening now may seem messy, confusing, slow, banal, frightening, but . . . this is what even the most revered and catalogued historical periods would have felt like when they were actually happening" (de Botton and Armstrong 2013, 194).

De Botton and Armstrong make a similar point about our own one-day-at-a-time experience of work: "it is likely to feel repetitive, uninspired, inadequately appreciated and under-paid, even when it is entirely worthwhile and on course" (de Botton and Armstrong 2013, 194). Work that you choose because you believe that eventually it will be rewarding to you and contribute to society may not always be fun.

The economy requires a vision of both/and rather than either/or. Can we be cautiously optimistic and at the same time recognize that work is hard and that it is not easy to evaluate our own historical moment? Yes, we can and we must. We appeal to family wisdom. Families are where we can talk about the tension between important work goals and feeling burned out moment to moment. Our families challenge us to work toward our aspirations, precisely because we need their help and support to do so. Some of our ideas may be controversial. We'll ask you to hear us out—and then talk about all these things with your own family network and the people you know.

Chapter Twenty-Five

Tempered Optimism, Humane Prosperity

This chapter begins by reviewing the connection between markets and innovation. It continues by making a connection between family wisdom and a particularly significant choice, finding or creating your life's work. At its best, family wisdom leads us to find or create work we love. We then combine these ideas into a model of a tempered and humane economy.

Markets are the basic "iron ore" of a humane economy, yes, tempered as suggested in the previous section, but the market principle is the foundation for the virtuous circle between prosperity and innovation. In figure 25.1, increasing prosperity causes innovation and improvements in technology which then cause further increases in prosperity, innovation, prosperity, innovation, creating an upward spiral of innovation and prosperity.

The right hand arrow represents the investments that prosperity makes possible. People planning to open a new store or build a new production

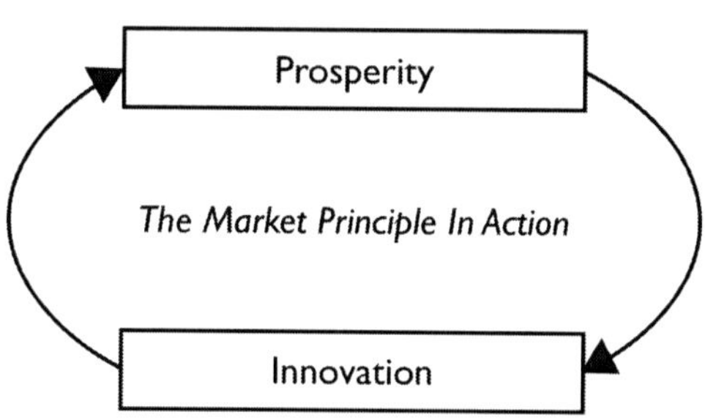

Figure 25.1. Market Virtuous Circle

(distribution, service) facility want to incorporate the best technology available. That creates a demand for innovation, encouraging both the garage inventor and the research and development departments of major corporations. Prosperity increases the investments in math and science that underlie major advances in technology—railroads and electricity and automobiles and transistors and smart phones, to barely scratch the surface.

The left hand arrow represents the goods and services created by innovation—which are themselves increases in prosperity. Sometimes prosperity is better phones or household appliances or cars. Sometimes prosperity is the richer set of choices between various goods and services that technology makes possible. You can call, text, email, or write your Mom for her birthday; you can jump in a car or on a plane to go see her. Sometimes innovation simply saves time—time that can be spent playing the banjo or flying kites with your grandkids. Sometimes the effects of innovation are not visible to consumers, but a new inventory method that simplifies logistics means money in someone's pocket. For a kind of shorthand we often measure prosperity in dollars, and innovation increases those measures too.

To complete the circle, as innovation increases prosperity it increases the income available to be used for more education, research and development, and so on, which in turn creates more innovation leading to still more prosperity. To create widespread prosperity the market virtuous circle requires the inclusive institutions we have thought about earlier.

Family wisdom is also essential, and it creates a virtuous circle of its own—although exactly how will take a bit more explaining. Following the lead of economics in general, until this point in the book we have assumed consumption and investment were mutually exclusive—as if an hour spent working was by definition an hour you are not consuming. But now we'd like to challenge that notion.

Think about someone in the prime years of his career, perhaps a person who makes hand-carved furniture. Let's imagine he chose that line of work because he loves it and has a gift for it. You could say that he is simultaneously working, consuming, and investing. Working is self-evident; he plans to sell the furniture to earn his income. As for consuming, what economists mean by the term is you're doing something that gives you pleasure while meeting your wants and needs. Even though he plans to sell the front hall table he's working on today, working on it is still the exact thing he wants to do. As for investing, making himself more productive, it is easy to imagine that the more furniture he makes the better he will get at it. He is honing his carpentry skills in the process of choosing the wood, the equipment, figuring out the exact cuts and joins, and so forth. The people who work with him, apprentices perhaps, also benefit from his experience and discoveries; he is investing in them as well.[1] It is easy to imagine he might spend some time outside the workshop with people in a similar line of work sharing discoveries they have made. He might even have a long running show on public television.[2]

Such a person would imagine a distinction between working, consuming, and investing to be quite artificial. For shorthand we call these "integrated" persons.[3] They go to work because that is what they want to do. The process of doing their work makes them more productive in the future. You can probably think of a dozen other examples: a fisherman in Homer, Alaska, for example, dipnetting for red salmon who says "something had come alive inside us . . . work was play."[4] Doctors basically want to see patients, read medical journals, and conduct research in their specialty. Professional athletes enjoy their sports and practice to improve. College professors enjoy reading the books and articles we plan to use in the classroom and in our research; we enjoy interacting with students.

Though they may not use the term, everyone prefers, and perhaps even deserves, to have a vocation that enables them to live as an integrated person. For families who are sufficiently prosperous there is a connection between being or becoming an integrated person and the family principle of using family resources to best meet the needs of family members. Figure 25.2 illustrates the way families operate at their best.

In the family diagram the right hand arrow is investment as it was in the market diagram, but this time we're specifically emphasizing families investing in family members. Families that live by the "respect abilities, respect needs" principle invest in their children to help them become integrated individuals. For middle and upper income families, that is a large part of what higher education is about. Chapter 10 spoke of the way we diversify our investment in our children—in everyday language, give them the opportunity to discover their own gifts and abilities. Chapter 2 reminded us that the family economy involves a network, people who do not necessarily live in your house, and chapter 11 reminded us of the need to invest in those children as well, although there certainly are problems as we discussed.

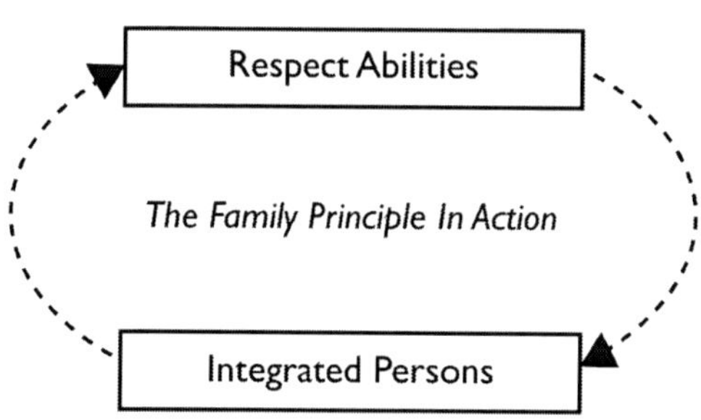

Figure 25.2. Family Virtuous Circle

The left hand arrow represents mentoring—imparting family wisdom. The life experiences of integrated individuals have taught them the value of good and rewarding work. Integrated people have greater self-respect and more respect for others. Children who grow up in a household of integrated adults have a much different world view than those who don't. You can think of this arrow, mentoring, as the thing that integrated persons "produce" and give to family members. Family wisdom creates its own virtuous circle, the principle of respect fostering the development of integrated persons through family investment in education and mentoring.

If you compare this circle with the earlier market one you'll notice that here the causation arrows are dashed rather than solid. We used solid lines for the market diagram because at this point in history most people would agree that a virtuous circle between innovation and prosperity exists. It's simply a fact. On the other hand, the idea of a family virtuous circle is new, somewhat speculative. We observe it in our students and their families, our colleagues and their families, many of our friends and neighbors. But we cannot claim that all economists would agree that this family virtuous circle exists. In twenty years, a generation, our hope and prediction is that they will, but for now we're making the causation arrows dashed.

The appropriate mix of family and market principles creates our vision of an economy. Figure 25.3 reflects the argument that the market and family principles together create a larger virtuous circle, a tempered and humane economy.

By placing the market principle at the bottom we emphasize that markets are the base of a humane economy. The long left hand upward arrow connecting the market principle circle and the family principle circle is again a solid line. The prosperity produced by markets helps families. Greater resources mean more and more meaningful choices, improving the odds of writing the great American novel if that is where your passion leads you. You can do better by your children. Recall that Levitt and Dubner found strong evidence that the most important determinants of a child's educational success are the parents' prosperity and education. This arrow essentially argues that the "product" of markets, what they create at their best, is functional families where people are respected and encouraged to live as integrated persons.

Gladwell makes the startling argument that markets may create integrated persons, even when the market conditions themselves are nothing like optimal. While completely acknowledging the harsh conditions in the garment trade in New York around 1900, he argues that it provided meaningful work for many recent immigrants from Eastern Europe because the work had "autonomy, complexity, and a connection between effort and reward" (Gladwell 2008, 149). The latter is exactly the market principle. Such work, he

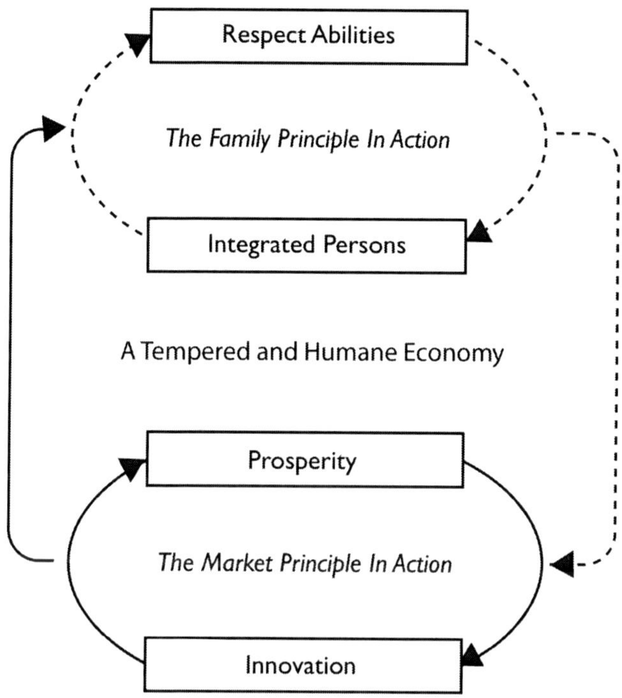

Figure 25.3. A Tempered and Humane Economy

argued, was a way-station to an integrated job—for the next generation. This is the argument we are making, except we hope that by now many people do not have to wait a generation to get the job they love.

Some people have worried that as people get jobs they love there won't be anybody left to do the sort of jobs nobody loves. Our model suggests that the answer is essentially technology. To pick an extreme example, there was a time when we'd guess no one loved being a garbage man. Because of improvements in technology, in our neighborhoods now the garbage man never has to leave the truck cab. If no one loves being a garbage man, perhaps at least some don't hate it, and those involved certainly know how important their services are to their communities.

There is one more long arrow in the diagram, that going down from the family principle circle to the market principle circle. It is dashed and tentative, but the suggestion is that as families are better able to live by the family principle, the economy will become more prosperous. In one way our argument is simple. Integrated persons living in functional families are more productive, more creative and innovative, and work harder than those who merely tolerate or hate their jobs. They are "invested" in their jobs. Chapter

21 argues that some people might prefer to work in business rather than in the nonprofit sector because they believe market discipline, as compared to family discipline, will prompt them to realize their best and most creative selves—to do good and meaningful work. Here we need only to make the connection between functional families and the hopes and expectations we bring to the workplace. When your best self has been routinely fostered at home, you will bring more to the workplace and expect more from it. Family expectations are the fire that tempers a market economy.

Earlier in the book we thought about families deciding whether to buy a video game or take a college class, implicitly assuming the former is consumption and the latter investment. But some recent developments are creating new possibilities. As Sharon Begley reported in the *Smithsonian* (July-August 2014, 15) "a growing community of scientists and engineers is borrowing the elements that make video or computer games so addictive—rewards, points, leaderboards and online collaboration—to enlist thousands of players to solve legitimate scientific mysteries." In one case medical researchers were attempting to map the configuration of an enzyme important to finding a cure for AIDS. They had used their standard computer algorithm methods diligently over several years, but failed to solve the problem. Someone had the inspiration of seeking the help of young adults with expertise in online 3-D puzzles. They created a game called "Foldit" in which players compete and collaborate in predicting the structure of a protein-cutting enzyme. The gamers made enough progress in three weeks that the scientists could go ahead and solve the problem.[5] This kind of research has the potential for many exciting applications.[6]

Prosperity helps put video games within the reach of many households in society. Family members acquire skills that may cycle back into the economy, facilitating the innovation and technology virtuous circle. If some gamers turn out to be medical researchers so much the better. Video games as investment—the world is a surprising place. This is a cautionary tale for those that are worried about the negative effect of technology on the next generation. In the modern world human brains and electronic ones work in concert, each relying on and helping the other. Those who need a little more convincing can watch the TED talk by Jane McGonigal "Gaming Can Make a Better World." Technology will increasingly allow society to draw on the wisdom of large numbers of people.

To argue as we have done that society may become more prosperous over time does not mean of course that everyone will become more prosperous; life has too many ups and downs for that. The important question is whether all income levels will experience an increase in prosperity.

Those at the top of the income distribution will certainly get richer. What about those in the middle? The highly respected economist Tyler Cowen, whose previous work we have already cited, recently argued there is cause for concern for the middle class. He says that in the future income will be earned by people who do the best job of providing the human half of human-technology collaboration. That's similar to the argument we're making. But he says that middle class persons will increasingly be unable to thrive as the human half of those teams. There we part company. We see no reason why members of the middle class in striving to be integrated persons, and in helping their children do the same, will be left behind interacting with technology. We've used video games to illustrate what we mean. Cowen himself provides some relevant data (2013, 20–21). Unmanned drones are a new technology compared to F-16 fighter aircraft. Both require many hours of support by technology staff on the ground. But, depending on their size, the drones require 168 or 300 hours of tech support for an hour in the air; the F-16 fewer than 100. This is a case where improving technology is creating middle income jobs, rather than the reverse.

One of our particular concerns has been the ability of families in the lower sections of the income distribution to make formal and informal investments in themselves. Actually we see a reason for measured optimism here as well. It is our view that differences in income do not systematically affect the "respect abilities, respect needs" principle. Families of all incomes share this principle; it's just that the constraints on a family's decision making depend crucially on the level of prosperity. The same principle that leads the poor to not invest, because other needs have priority, leads the prosperous to invest. If we are right about the overall increasing prosperity of the economy, then as the prosperity of any given family improves over the generations, they may well invest more in each child, because increasing prosperity is almost always associated with a lower birth rate. Once basic needs are met, many families identify investing in the next generation as their most important priority and so for each child there will be more resources available.

We also remember that families toward the bottom of the income distribution often cast a wide net when defining who counts as family. Although that restricts their ability to invest in others when the family is very poor, it also means investment can become more widespread as incomes increase. Just as the extended family sometimes patches income from a number of network members together to make the rent, as they become more prosperous they might patch together funds for tuition or a business license. While no one can become complacent, we believe that people of all income groups can put themselves in a position to improve their prosperity.

The goal is a humane economy; tempering productive markets with family wisdom is the means. The figure of speech helps articulate our two main ideas. Markets need tempering to create a flexible and robust economy, and our relationships with those we love best are a great model for creating the institutions that both support and temper markets. A humane economy serves all different kinds of people, so we use the metaphor of a well tempered musical instrument that allows for composition in all major and minor keys. Designing the tuning system, tuning the instrument, not to mention actually playing, require that musicians have great knowledge, perhaps even a kind of wisdom. A humane economy is tuned to provide widespread prosperity.

Creating a humane economy requires many collective decisions and we needn't get them all right the first time. No major feature of our society was ever achieved at a single stroke—think of the move from the Articles of Confederation to the Constitution, or the century between the Civil War and the Civil Rights Movement. We believe that there are good reasons for tempered optimism because our country will get things right often enough. Over the long haul, a country which gets things right 60 percent of the time will create humane prosperity more often than one which gets things right only half the time, let alone one that gets things wrong more often than not. Because of what we know about markets and families, we'll get things right often enough. Increasingly we will realize the benefits of a tempered and humane economy.

NOTES

1. In the past many people were apprentices. Now secondary and post-secondary education has to fill that role, aided by practicums, internships, service learning programs, and the like. Advocates of such programs claim that "work integrated learning provides universities with the opportunity to graduate students with the capacity to integrate the theory learned in the classroom and the practice learned in the workplace to problem-solve difficult and complex matters in their lives and as part of their work" (Cooper, Orrell, and Bowden 2010, 189). An unexpected advantage of such programs is that they may help students avoid professions in which they would not become integrated persons. Until her high school work-study program, one of Pat's daughters thought she would become a kindergarten teacher, but she became a CPA instead.
2. Such a person is Roy Underhill who gave up life as a teacher and thirty-three years later is still hosting *The Woodwright's Shop*, a favorite show of Pat's son-in-law.
3. That people might or should get as much life satisfaction from their work as from any other activity they do is certainly not new with us. As far as we are aware, we are the ones to introduce the term "integrated person." Jannett has argued elsewhere that Bradley University, where we work, was founded on the principles of the Arts and Crafts Movement associated with William Morris and John Ruskin. There she argues the Arts and Crafts movement believed that "work should be pleasurable, that workers should be artists, that production and design should be inseparable" (Highfill 1998, 31). Our notion of an integrated person does not have, however, an anti-industrialism connotation.
4. This example is from Miranda Weiss (2009, 108) *Tide, Feather, Snow*.
5. This story is told by Leila Gray in the University of Washington alumni magazine, September 19, 2011. http://www.washington.edu/news/2011/09/19/gamers-succeed-where-scientists-fail/. The scientific results can be found in Khatib, Firas et al. 2011. "Crystal Structure of a Monomeric Retroviral Protease Solved by Protein Folding Game Players." *Nature Structural & Molecular Biology* 18: 1175–77.
6. The game "EyeWire," for example, is used to help study how mammals detect motion. Kim, Jinseop S. et al. 2014. "Space-time Wiring Specificity Supports Direction Selectivity in the Retina." *Nature* 509: 331–36.

Appendix 1

When You Have Enough to Share, Share Wisely

Were you ever told as a child to eat your supper because of all the starving children in the world? If this happened to you, or if you can imagine it, you probably did care about those kids. You may well have wondered what you could do about it. At an early age you figured out that shipping your leftovers to another country is unrealistic, so you knew there was a disconnect between "eat your broccoli" and helping others. What about clothing for the poor? You can ship used clothes abroad, but should you?[1]

In the tough love section we mentioned Lupton's insights into things we can do to help those in other countries. One of his major themes is a note of caution. He tells the story of a pastor in Nicaragua. Lupton asked him about how effective help from American churches was at mitigating poverty in his area. After much prodding the pastor, Juan,

> went on to describe how entrepreneurship declines as dollars and free resources flood in, how people become conditioned to wait for the next mission group to arrive instead of building their businesses through their own efforts. He talked about how dignity is eroded as people come to view themselves as charity cases for wealthy visitors, how they pose with smiling faces for pictures to be taken back for the marketing of the next group. "They are turning my people into beggars," Juan said, now with full emotion. . . .
>
> But Juan did not blame them for becoming beggars. He faulted the affluent, well-meaning U.S. churches for their unexamined generosity. His accusations, now pouring forth with considerable force, were directed at the naïve "vacationaries" spending millions of dollars traveling to his country, creating a welfare economy that deprives people of the pride of their own accomplishments. (Lupton 2011, 20–21)

The basic idea is that we should be wise in helping others, taking incentives into account the way Church Mouse stores do in this country. As an object lesson and more positive example, Lupton also tells the stories of two water wells built in Central America. In a Honduran village a North American church hired well-drilling engineers to build the well, and when it broke down the villagers simply waited for church people to come fix it. In a Nicaraguan village, the North American organization Opportunity International of Chicago provided a micro loan and a community developer to help the villagers set up a local water company and hire a reliable Nicaraguan engineer. The villagers provided some savings, all the labor, and the village now owns its own water company, a source of both pride and income (Lupton 2011, 12–13).

Many families we know have a passion and commitment to helping people in need wherever they are in the world. But families at their best also know a lot about the art of the possible. On her way to a meeting Jannett happened to take the Orange Line from Midway Airport to the Loop in Chicago. A food bank had purchased one of those overhead poster ads that said: "If everyone in Chicago were to donate one can of food, one hour of their time, or one dollar, we would no longer have a hunger problem in Chicago." So Jannett came home to talk to Pat about it. Sure the ad was just trying to encourage more people to get involved, but suppose all Chicagoans really did. The logistics would be overwhelming. How would they collect the cans? Where would they store them? Anyone who has ever coordinated a volunteer event knows that it is a formidable task organizing a hundred volunteers, let alone a thousand or tens of thousands. The food bank must have some organizational geniuses on board if they think they can be good stewards of the resources they are asking for.

The essential problem is not the lack of good intentions. A good proportion of the households in Chicago would be happy to give a dollar, an hour, or a can of food if they thought it would help. In fact, we suspect many households would give a lot more if they thought there would be real long run benefits for the malnourished in the city. In a rich country like ours the essential economic problem is coordination, putting all those resources to work.

When people find out we're interested in this topic we often hear their strongly expressed opinions. We have friends that are adamantly against an increased role of the government in anything. Well, if these people have a heart for the poor they will have to rely on private means. They can volunteer at places like the Peoria Friendship House, for example, a settlement house in our city with programs to help children do better in school, help single mothers become more employable, and help people with language difficulties. How much time you should devote to investing in the poor depends on your circumstances. And frankly, it often depends on where you are in your life cycle, young, middle aged, or getting on in life. Young people must invest in themselves, the middle aged in themselves, their children, and often their grandchildren. But at some point in your life cycle you should turn serious attention to investing in the world at large. You can prepare yourself for that just as you do for other aspects of retirement. You can investigate what the volunteer opportunities in your community are; you can take classes on how to teach English as a second language; you can simply make a commitment to do something.

And just as we have argued that people should be integrated persons during their working life, they should strive to be integrated in helping others. We have a colleague who finds ways of helping her daughter with her homework that they both enjoy. Helping with homework is investing, of course, but it is also consumption for both parties to the extent that it gives them pleasure. Just as it is wise and appropriate to encourage college students to find the vocation that lets them live an integrated and joyful life, it is appropriate for you to find a helping avocation you enjoy. Human nature being what it is, once you find a possible activity, reading to children in an after school program for example, commit yourself for a period of time, a school year or a semester. Give yourself a chance to get used to where to park, how to prepare, what to do for lunch, and the personalities of the people you're around. After having given it a chance, if you find that it's not for you, try something else.

At the most practical level we want to go back again to Paul Tough's *How Children Succeed*. His main idea has two parts. (1) Children's success depends as much on non-cognitive skills as on cognitive ones. (2) Non-cognitive skills like "grit, curiosity, self-control, and optimism" can be taught (Tough 2012, 122, 196 and elsewhere). Clearly as teachers we believe in the value of education. But his ideas suggest that what most young people in the lower reaches of the income distribution need most is not necessarily the province of traditional teachers. Mentors are as important for their caring as for their "tutoring" help. We suspect people who are financially in a position to help the less fortunate know a lot that they can share about the "grit, curiosity, self-control, and optimism" Paul Tough discusses. That may be what you have to give. You can teach a child to read—but if that isn't your strength you can simply mentor the child, help her find her path through life. Teach her the same things you taught the children in your own life. Become one of the mentors Elana believes are needed for the children in her neighborhood. Your religious home, local school, or an organization like the Boys and Girls Club in your community can help match you with a child.

We've been talking about volunteer activities in the not-for-profit sector. But we also have friends who are strongly of the view that the government is a good way to achieve our goals. People with this philosophy will at a minimum vote their beliefs. They will lobby and inform themselves about what the government is already doing, perhaps with an eye to what more the government might do. Their responsibility is to make sure that the government is being a good steward of our tax money. The essential problem, as we see it, is one of program design. That is, the government does not have a magic wand that solves the coordination problem. If a food bank in Chicago persuaded the city government to pass a law requiring everyone to give one hour, one dollar, or one can of food, the practical problems would be just as difficult as if all Chicagoans voluntarily responded to the overhead poster ad for the food bank.

Some people may decide the best thing they can do to help the poor is the painstaking science of investigating whether modest incentive programs really work, for example, whether giving children phone minutes for reading helps comprehension, or whether a new corn hybrid is pest resistant in specific soil and moisture conditions. In fact, we would argue that designing programs that really help the poor in the long run must confront the hard questions that scientists ask. A related problem is that good science requires good data. For example, much of the recent scientific evidence about the relationship of prosperity to child well-being comes from European studies because the United States does not have good panel data sets. Good intentions notwithstanding, it is science that investigates the question of what works and what doesn't.

Entrepreneurship and innovation are also essential. Just as innovation is the engine for increasing overall prosperity, it can be the engine for helping those at the lower end of the income distribution. Many people have found quite creative ways to get help to the poor in a functional way. Heifer International, for example, has a well thought out plan of how the offspring from an animal given to an individual family can be distributed through the community. For another example, the firm Vestergaard Frandsen has developed a "LifeStraw" that reduces the terrible effects of unclean drinking water. The device is being distributed by both for-profit and not-for-profit enterprises. The innovation is the technology of water purification, but it is also in the design of the program, and notice that there is nothing that says investing in the poor has to be charity. If you're creative enough you might think of a way to both support yourself and invest in the poor.

Most of the examples here and in the next appendix are not things that we have done ourselves. Our friends give us information about organizations they believe in. One great thing about innovative ideas is that they spread like wildfire. A great product or design will be copied. Governments get their program design ideas from somewhere. A good water delivery system, playground equipment designed for the dual purpose of drawing water from a well and giving the kids a safe place to play, might be copied by many local governments in places that need good drinking water for the citizens. (See appendix 2.)

As is perhaps clear by now we want everyone to consider spending time helping those around them. That kind of help can be ad hoc, or you can work through an organized charity. For those people who can't give time to helping others because of family responsibilities or their own health situation—those people might give money. How much time or money, of course, depends on their circumstances. But we would argue that you should at least invest the time and care necessary to figure out how your time and/or money is best spent. For some people who know only too well specific individuals who could benefit from a little help, getting the kids into school this year, for example, it may be easy to figure out what to do. For people acting through a charity, their first job is to research the charity itself. What does it do? Perhaps that means a mission statement, but it certainly means finding out what the "boots on the ground" actually do. How does it raise funds? How are they spent? We ourselves prefer some smaller charities that don't have elaborate bookkeeping and fundraising departments and where we can know the players themselves. In any event, we ask you to strive for an appropriate balance between information gathering and getting on with helping people. Appendix 2 may help you get started.

NOTE

1. The global export of used clothing generates millions of dollars of revenue, whether it is done by for profit business or not-for-profit agencies. In Africa, in particular, the increase in used clothes sales since the early 1980s has coincided with a decline in the local clothing industry. So far establishing a causal relationship between those two trends is beyond the reach of economic analysis (Brooks and Simon 2012).

Appendix 2

Concrete Suggestions for Sharing

In response to a question from his wife about which charities they should support Stephen Smith, development economist from George Washington University, wrote a book we admire: *Ending Global Poverty: A Guide to What Works* (2005). He categorizes the "poverty traps" that the world's poor fall into, and gives suggestions of organizations trying to help people escape from these traps. This appendix and Smith's ideas do not substitute for doing your own due diligence, but they might give you some ideas about where to start. Among Smith's ideas are:

1. Health and nutrition problems: safe water projects such as the Roundabout Playpump now under Water for People (waterforpeople.org); the AIDS Support Organization (tasouganda.org) (Smith 2005, 49–50, 52–54).
2. Lack of basic education: Pratham (prathamusa.org), working in India focusing on basic education; BRAC (brac.net), the Bangladesh Rural Advancement Committee with programs covering most of the traps listed here; Save the Children (savethechildren.net) which is highly rated by both the American Institute of Philanthropy and Charity Navigator (Smith 2005, 61–63, 65–67, 70–74).
3. Lack of credit and insurance possibilities: Grameen Bank (grameenfoundation.org) mentioned in the text; The Foundation of International Community Assistance (globalmarketplace.org), focusing more specifically on poverty reduction than other microfinance institutions; Project Hope (projecthope.org), which integrates health with finance; Kiva (kiva.org) (Smith 2005, 75–79, 79–82, 82–84). Kiva is not in Smith, but seems especially relevant; please see chapter 19.

4. Market Development: BRAC again, but with a special program for the "ultra-poor"; Self-Employed Women's Association in India (sewa.org); Kerala Dinesh Beedi Workers Central Co-op Society (keraladinesh.com), a self-organized worker co-op network in India (Smith 2005, 89–97, 100–102).
5. Problems of access to new technologies: Small Enterprise Assistance Fund (globalhand.org), a non-profit which invests in small businesses through for-profit investment funds; the Same Language Subtitling (iimahd.ernet.in), a system for teaching literacy through popular songs which won a grant from the R J Matthai Center for Educational Innovation in India; TechnoServe (technoserve.org), a top-rated non-governmental organization which focuses on product improvement and market development (Smith 2005, 103–6, 110, 111–14).
6. Environmental degradation: "Africa Now Kisumu" (wiser.org), Kenya, which has brought bee-keeping to the poor, improving their income with honey and increasing cross-pollination which has improved crop production; FUNDECOR (amigosofcostarica.org) in Costa Rica, working to save local forests by helping the poor find other ways of producing income rather than deforesting their land; Heifer International (heifer.org) in Lima, Peru, working in an urban environment changing a slum into a community (Smith 2005, 115–17, 121–22, 123–26).
7. Social inclusion and human rights: Childline India Foundation (childlineindia.org), a hotline for children in trouble; Cambodian League for the Promotion and Defense of Human Rights (licadho-cambodia.org) (Smith 2005, 130–31, 132–33).
8. Community empowerment and development: World Vision (wvi.org), helping to organize mother's clubs and youth programs, providing job training and a chance for further education for some; Africare (africare.org), working in areas others have not dared, with a highly rated program (Smith 2005, 143–45, 148–53).

Some of these problems require political changes, but they are also being addressed by these organizations and others that are similar. We have observed previously that the best organizations tackle both the need to feed people and the need to teach them to fish. Many do so in quite innovative ways.

As we have mentioned, a personal favorite of ours is Heifer International. This is an organization that helps farmers on every continent except Antarctica improve their productive capabilities through gifts of animals and instruction in their care. The animals are carefully chosen to suit the climate and terrain, running from hives of bees to water buffalo or camels and all sizes between. One of their slogans is "Heifer International doesn't feed families.

We empower families to feed themselves." What we like about the program is "passing on the gift" where each farmer receiving an animal is expected to give an offspring and instruction to a neighbor so the gift spreads throughout the community.

Another organization balancing meeting immediate needs with encouraging participation in the market sector is Water Step (waterstep.org). It is "an international organization that protects the lives of nearly 400,000 people each year by providing training and equipment to individuals seeking to address water quality and sanitation issues in developing countries and post-disaster environments." Estimates are that more people die of waterborne disease than cancer or HIV/AIDS. Recently the Development Council of Morton, IL, initiated a program to collect 4,000 pairs of shoes to be donated to the Shoes for Water program. EDGE Outreach (edgeoutreach.com), parent organization of Water Step, sells the 25,000 to 30,000 pairs collected each month at low prices to micro business owners to resell to people in the same country where there are water projects. This helps the small businesses both to provide a sustainable income for their families and to get shoes on the feet of many who would otherwise be barefoot and suffer from foot abrasions and parasites. The revenue collected from shoe sales by EDGE Outreach pays for the water equipment and training in the same communities where the new shoe businesses are created.

Smaller more impromptu efforts can also be effective. A neighbor of Pat's told her that her religious congregation asked a missionary what the most important thing was that they could do to improve the lives of the people in the community where he worked. He said to help them get a well so they could have clean water and not have to spend many hours a day bringing water from a not-so-clean stream a few miles away. They quickly organized a collection and soon had enough funds to build both a well and a school. These efforts can be quite effective as long as the cautionary notes we talked about in appendix 1 are kept in mind.

Efforts to help the poor can involve for-profit firms. "LifeStraw" is a straw that allows people to drink water that is otherwise not potable. Google the name. http://www.vestergaard-frandsen.com/lifestraw. There's a picture of a child drinking cloudy water through the straw that is bigger than an ordinary straw, but not unmanageable. It's essentially a low cost portable water filter packaged in a convenient way. There is a benefit to the environment as well because the families would otherwise have to burn firewood to purify the water.

Pat also wants to especially mention her personal favorite of Smith's suggestions, one which was new to her, the Roundabout Playpump. It is an old-fashioned merry-go-round like we have in schoolyards, powered by children's feet but pumping water up from a well to supply the village. Jannett especially wants to mention Bridges to Prosperity (http://bridgestoprosperity.org/), an organization that builds footbridges in rural areas because these people often live in a walking world. When a river floods, getting to work or school or the doctor becomes impossible. Footbridges improve access to markets and improve lives.

A program that balances immediate help with training for improving future productivity is Dress for Success, Peoria, one of 119 affiliates of a worldwide program (dressforsuccess.org) operating in twelve countries. The women served are referred to the agency by homeless shelters, job training programs, the immigration service, and other nonprofit groups. They practice interview techniques, receive interview attire, advice on hair and accessories, and help with resumes. On obtaining employment the women are given a week's worth of appropriate clothing and become part of the Professional Women's Group where there are classes in four main topics: written rules of the workplace, unwritten rules of the workplace, financial literacy, and health and wellness. Over 70 percent of the more than 1,500 women who have been served in Peoria have found employment; many of them are single mothers, hoping for a better life for themselves and their children. One of their many success stories is Catalina, the Hispanic outreach coordinator at Peoria Friendship House of Christian Service, who won the Valeska S. Hinton Human Rights Award. She helps immigrants fill out citizenship papers and has conducted workshops that help U.S. citizens get their immigration questions answered. She goes with community members to the hospital, doctors appointments, dental visits, the employment office, and court hearings to help as a translator if needed.

Don't forget Boys and Girls Clubs which offer programs in many cities. Among the things they offer are tutoring programs emphasizing school success and mentoring programs to provide positive role models. They attempt to teach values such as resistance to the risk-taking behaviors of substance abuse and gang activities, stressing personal responsibility. These organizations and many similar ones try to instill some of that grit, curiosity, and character Paul Tough stresses. And if you want to be inspired by a boy who has character, read about Joshua's Heart Foundation (joshuasheart.org) to learn what a five-year-old boy started because he cared about the poor. As reported by Joe Kita (December 2, 2012) in *Parade* his organization has given away 400,000 pounds of food and has a backpack program which issues food to children for weekends when they don't get food at school. As we mentioned in chapter 3, a child whose brain is busy worrying about being hungry can't learn.

As is certainly evident, we have a special interest in education. Part of the bad luck of the poor is that they must live in areas where the schools are relatively poor. Think back to Elana in chapter 2, and remember that although she can't afford the time or money to continue her own schooling, she is determined that her grandson will succeed in school. Partly to make up for a shortage of such grandmothers in Peoria, the local school district has implemented a program for third graders called Reading Buddies. In the 2011–2012 school year there were 450 volunteers who enabled 255 students to have a one-on-one tutoring experience each week. Not surprisingly these buddies included retired teachers and parents. The pleasant surprise was that members of the CEO Roundtable of the Chamber of Commerce, recognizing their need for educated workers, sponsored teams of their employees so that each team member would come once a month, but the child would have someone from the same team each week. According to Renee McKinnon, Instructional Improvement Officer, District 150, Peoria, Illinois, the program is being expanded because of its success (Personal Communication).

A dozen or so concerned citizens in Peoria gathered a few years ago to explore ways they could help the children in poorer areas be more successful in school. Believing that reading is the key to success, reading quickly became the focus. LOOK, IT'S MY BOOK (lookitsmybook.org) is a completely grass roots organization, largely made up of retired persons recruited through the continuing education program of Bradley University. Funded by donations and occasional fund-raisers, they began with one school, giving children in kindergarten through fourth grade brand new books to own, books they chose themselves from age appropriate selections. The program has expanded to ten schools, with the distributions now happening six times a year. A church has donated storage space, there is a captain who recruits volunteers for each distribution, and the program has been enthusiastically received by both the children and their teachers. So far over 50,000 books have been given to children, many of whom have few books in their homes.

Another program in Peoria that is achieving success is called ELITE (eliteyp.org). There the target is older students to get them ready for the work force, teaching such basic skills as how to dress properly for a job interview and a job, how to write a resume, appropriate interviewing behavior, the importance of showing up on time, and respect for others. Sponsored through the Peoria Park District and working through the schools, ELITE helps these students find part-time jobs so they can practice the skills they are learning and, in some cases, find mentors who may help them move on with their education or into better jobs. ELITE also works with adults through a program called RE-Entry to help find jobs for ex-felons and teach them the value of respect and commitment.

After school programs at churches and nonprofit social agencies have also seen the need for tutoring that poor families are unable to provide. Many part-time and retired teachers have volunteered to help in these programs. One agency we know uses college students who are education majors at schools nearby to work with children on a one-to-one basis, again providing a much needed role model for the children. The focus there is on basic skills, getting homework done, and often the programs cover all subjects and all eight grades of primary school.

Ask at your local library or your local school if there is some program where you can be of help. If you ask, you'll probably find several. If you are among the lucky, there is an unlucky person somewhere you can help.

Acknowledgments

A long manuscript requires the help and support of many people. We are most grateful to our first readers, Sondra Callahan, Tracy Harris, Lois Hill, Shondra Johnson, Kathleen Kirk, Michael McAsey, Kevin O'Brien, Linda Parsons, Ray Wojcikewych, and Janice Zacardo. The book was immeasurably improved by Richard Gretz, Elana Linwood, and William Weber. Special thanks go to Mary Blank, Karla Layne, and Catalina Zavala. Lois Hill graciously compiled the index.

We are also most grateful for the help and support of our editor Joseph C. Parry, Lexington Books.

Bibliography

Acemoglu, Daron and James A. Robinson. 2012. *Why Nations Fail: The Origins of Power, Prosperity, and Poverty*. New York: Crown, Crown Business.

Adams, John C. and Ken B. Cyree. 2004. "Market Efficiency and Diversification: An Experimental Approach Using the Wall Street Journal's Dartboard Portfolio." *Journal of Applied Finance* 14 (2): 40–51.

Adler, Mortimer J. 1991. *Desires Right and Wrong: The Ethics of Enough*. New York: Macmillan.

Akee, Randall K. Q., William E. Copeland, Gordon Keeler, Adrian Angold, and E. Jane Costello. 2010. "Parents' Incomes and Children's Outcomes: A Quasi-Experiment using Transfer Payments from Casino Profits." *American Economic Journal: Applied Economics* 2 (1): 86–115.

Alesina, Alberto, Reza Baqir, and William Easterly. 1999. "Public Goods and Ethnic Divisions." *Quarterly Journal of Economics* 114 (4): 1243–84.

Annim, Samuel Kobina. 2012. "Microfinance Efficiency: Trade-Offs and Complementarities between the Objectives of Microfinance Institutions and their Performance Perspectives." *European Journal of Development Research* 24 (5): 788–807.

Ariely, Dan. 2008. *Predictably Irrational: The Hidden Forces That Shape Our Decisions*. New York: Harper.

Becker, Gary S. 1991. *A Treatise on the Family (Enlarged Edition)*. Cambridge, MA: Harvard University Press.

Bernheim, B. Douglas, Andrei Shleifer, and Lawrence H. Summers. 1986. "The Strategic Bequest Motive." *Journal of Labor Economics* 4 (3): S151–S182.

Beshears, John, James Choi, David Laibson, Brigitte Madrian, and Jung Sakon. 2011. *Self Control and Liquidity: How to Design a Commitment Contract*. RAND Corporation Publications Department, Working Papers: 895.

Bitler, Marianne P. and Hilary W. Hoynes. 2010. "The State of the Social Safety Net in the Post-Welfare Reform Era." *Brookings Papers on Economic Activity*: 71–127.

Borcherding, Thomas E. and Darren Filson. 2002. "Group Consumption, Free-Riding, and Informal Reciprocity Agreements." *Journal of Economic Behavior and Organization* 47 (3): 237–57.

Brooks, Andrew and David Simon. 2012. "Unravelling the Relationships between Used-Clothing Imports and the Decline of African Clothing Industries." *Development and Change* 43 (6): 1265–90.

Bruni, Luigino. 2012. *The Wound and the Blessing: Economics, Relationships, and Happiness*. Trans. N. Michael Brennen. Hyde Park, NY: New City Press.

Cerra, Valerie and Sweta Chaman Saxena. 2008. "Growth Dynamics: The Myth of Economic Recovery." *American Economic Review* 98 (1): 439–57.

Chingos, Matthew M. 2013. "Class Size and Student Outcomes: Research and Policy Implications." *Journal of Policy Analysis and Management* 32 (2): 411–38.

Clark, Don P., Jannett Highfill, Jonas de Oliveira Campino, and Scheherazade S. Rehman, 2011. "FDI, Technology Spillovers, Growth, and Income Inequality: A Selective Survey." *Global Economy Journal,* 11 (2): article 1.

Clement, Douglas. 2014, June. "Interview with Glenn Loury." *The Region* 28 (2).

Clement, Douglas. 2013, June. "Accounting for Job Loss." *The Region* 27 (2).

Clement, Douglas. 2011, September. "Interview with Daron Acemoglu." *The Region* 25 (3).

Colander, David C. 2013. *Economics*, 9th ed. New York: McGraw-Hill Irwin.

Cooper, Lesley, Janice Orrell, and Margaret Bowden. 2010. *Work Integrated Learning: A Guide to Effective Practice*. London and New York: Routledge.

Cowen, Tyler. 2013. *Average Is Over: Powering America Beyond The Age Of The Great Stagnation*. New York: Dutton.

Cowen, Tyler. 2012. *An Economist Gets Lunch: New Rules for Everyday Foodies*. New York: Dutton.

Cullity, Garrett. 2004. *The Moral Demands of Affluence*. Oxford: Clarendon Press

Dave, Dhaval M., Hope Corman, and Nancy E. Reichman. 2012. "Effects of Welfare Reform on Education Acquisition of Adult Women." *Journal of Labor Research* 33 (2): 251–82.

de Botton, Alain and John Armstrong. 2013. *Art as Therapy*. New York: Phaidon.

Eckes, Jr. Alfred E. 2011. *The Contemporary Global Economy: A History Since 1980*. Chichester, West Sussex: Wiley-Blackwell.

Feige, Edgar L. and Richard Cebula. 2011. *America's Underground Economy: Measuring the Size, Growth and Determinants of Income Tax Evasion in the U.S.* MPRA Paper 29672, University Library of Munich, Germany.

Frank, Robert H. 1985. *Choosing the Right Pond: Human Behavior and the Quest for Status*. New York and Oxford: Oxford University Press.

Gladwell, Malcolm. 2013. *David and Goliath: Underdogs, Misfits, and the Art of Battling Giants*. New York: Little, Brown and Co.

Gladwell, Malcolm. 2008. *Outliers: The Story of Success*. New York: Little, Brown and Co.

Gorton, Gary and Andrew Metrick. 2012. "Getting Up to Speed on the Financial Crisis: A One-Weekend-Reader's Guide." *Journal of Economic Literature* 50 (1): 128–50.

Gretz, Richard T., Jannett Highfill, and Robert C. Scott. 2012. "R&D Subsidy Games: A Cost Sharing Approach Vs. Reward for Performance." *Journal of Technology Transfer* 37 (4): 385–403.

Hastings, Justine S. and Jeffrey M. Weinstein. 2008. "Information, School Choice, and Academic Achievement: Evidence from Two Experiments." *Quarterly Journal of Economics* 123 (4): 1373–1414.

Heilbrun, Carolyn G. 1988. *Writing a Woman's Life*. New York: Ballantine.

Highfill, Jannett. 1998. "Arts and Crafts at Bradley Polytechnic Institute: A Theory of Work." In *The University as Learning Community: Tradition, Innovation, Prospects*, edited by Timothy K. Conley, 30–46. Peoria, IL: Bradley University.

Highfill, Jannett and Michael McAsey. 1997. "Municipal Waste Management: Recycling and Landfill Space Constraints." *Journal of Urban Economics* 41 (1): 118–36.

Highfill, Jannett and Kevin O'Brien. 2014. *The Effect of Ethnic Diversity on Municipal Spending*. Working Paper.

Highfill, Jannett and Raymond Wojcikewych. 2011. "The U.S.-China Exchange Rate Debate: Using Currency Offer Curves." *International Advances in Economic Research* 17 (4): 386–96.

Hirschman, Albert O. 1989. "Having Opinions—One of the Elements of Well-being?" *American Economic Review* 79 (2): 75–79.

Hough, Douglas E. 2013. *Irrationality in Health Care: What Behavioral Economics Reveals About What We Do and Why.* Stanford, CA: Stanford University Press.

Kahneman, Daniel. 2011. *Thinking, Fast and Slow*. New York: Farrar, Straus and Giroux.

Kissane, Rebecca Joyce and Susan Clampet-Lundquist. 2012. "Social Ties, Social Support, and Collective Efficacy among Families from Public Housing in Chicago and Baltimore." *Journal of Sociology & Social Welfare* 39 (4): 157–81.

Kote, Anil Kumar B. and P. M. Honnakeri. 2012. "Impacts of Microfinance on Poverty Alleviation and the Empowerment of Women with Special Reference to Rural Women Empowerment and Entrepreneurship Development in India." *International Journal of Research in Commerce and Management* 3 (4): 51–54.

Krueger, Alan B. 2012, January 12. "The Rise and Consequence of Inequality in the United States," speech delivered to the Center for American Progress.

Laibson, David. 2010. "Tools: Behavioral Economics." In *The Heart of Teaching Economic: Lessons from Leading Minds*, edited by Simon W. Bowmaker. Cheltenham, UK, and Northampton, MA: Edward Elgar.

Laing, Derek. 2011. *Labor Economics: Introduction to Classic and the New Labor Economics*. New York: Norton.

Levitt, Steven D. and Stephen J. Dubner. 2009. *Superfreakonomics: Global Cooling, Patriotic Prostitutes, and Why Suicide Bombers Should Buy Life Insurance*. New York: William Morrow.

Levitt, Steven D. and Stephen J. Dubner. 2005. *Freakonomics: A Rogue Economist Explores the Hidden Side of Everything*. New York: William Morrow.

Levitt, Steven D., John A. List, Susanne Neckermann, and Sally Sadoff. 2012. *The Behavioralist Goes to School: Leveraging Behavioral Economics to Improve Educational Performance*. National Bureau of Economic Research, Inc, NBER Working Papers: 18165.

Lomborg, Bjorn. 2007. *Cool It: The Skeptical Environmentalist's Guide to Global Warming*. New York: Alfred A. Knopf.

Lupton, Robert D. 2011. *Toxic Charity: How Churches and Charities Hurt Those They Help (And How to Reverse It)*. New York: HarperOne.

Luttmer, Erzo F. P. 2001. "Group Loyalty and the Taste for Redistribution." *Journal of Political Economy* 109 (3): 500–528.

Martin, Megan C. and Koen Caminada. 2011. "Welfare Reform in the U.S.: A Policy Overview Analysis." *Poverty and Public Policy* 3 (1): article 8.

McLean, Bethany and Joe Nocera. 2010. *All the Devils are Here: The Hidden History of the Financial Crisis*. New York: Portfolio/Penguin.

Meer, Jonathan and Jeremy West. 2013. *Effects of the Minimum Wage on Employment Dynamics*. National Bureau of Economic Research, Inc, NBER Working Papers: 19262.

Melzer, Brian T. 2011. "The Real Costs of Credit Access: Evidence from the Payday Lending Market." *Quarterly Journal of Economics* 126 (1): 517–55.

Nasar, Sylvia. 2011. *Grand Pursuit: The Story of Economic Genius*. New York: Simon & Schuster.

Neumark, David and William Wascher. 2006. *Minimum Wages and Employment: A Review of Evidence from the New Minimum Wage Research*. National Bureau of Economic Research, Inc, NBER Working Papers: 12663.

Newell, Richard G., William A. Pizer, and Daniel Raimi. 2013. "Carbon Markets 15 Years After Kyoto: Lessons Learned, New Challenges." *Journal of Economic Perspectives* 27 (1): 123–46.

Nordhaus, William. 2013. *The Climate Casino: Risk, Uncertainty, and Economics for a Warming World*. New Haven and London: Yale University Press.

Organski, A. F. K. and Jacek Kugler. 1977. "The Costs of Major Wars: The Phoenix Factor." *American Political Science Review* 71 (4): 1347–66.

Pinker, Steven. 2012 (c2011). *The Better Angels of Our Nature: Why Violence Has Declined*. New York: Penguin.

Poterba, James M. 1997. "Demographic Structure and the Political Economy of Public Education." *Journal of Policy Analysis and Management* 16 (1): 48–66.

Roemer, John E. 2012. "On Several Approaches to Equality of Opportunity." *Economics and Philosophy* 28 (2): 165–200.

Röpke, Wilhelm. 1986 (c1958). *A Humane Economy: The Social Framework of the Free Market*. Trans. Elizabeth Henderson. Lanham, MD: University Press of America.

Sachs, Jeffrey D. 2008. *Common Wealth: Economics for a Crowded Planet*. New York: Penguin Press.

Schreiner, Mark and Jonathan Morduch. 2002. "Opportunities and Challenges for Microfinance in the United States." In *Replicating Microfinance in the United States*, edited by James H. Carr, Zhong Yi Tong. Washington, DC: Woodrow Wilson Center Press, 19–61.

Sen, Amartya. 1995 (c1992). *Inequality Reexamined*. Cambridge, MA: Harvard University Press.

Servon, Lisa J. 2002. "Fulfilling the Potential of the U.S. Microenterprise Strategy." In *Replicating Microfinance in the United States*, edited by James H. Carr, Zhong Yi Tong. Washington, DC: Woodrow Wilson Center Press, 169–90.

Shiller, Robert J. 2012. *Finance and the Good Society*. Princeton, NJ: Princeton University Press.

Singer, Peter. 2009. *The Life You Can Save: Acting Now to End World Poverty*. New York: Random House.

Smith, Stephen C. 2005. *Ending Global Poverty: A Guide to What Works*. New York: Palgrave Macmillan.

Stack, Carol B. 1974. *All Our Kin: Strategies for Survival in a Black Community*. New York: Harper & Row.

Stiglitz, Joseph E. 2012. *The Price of Inequality: How Today's Divided Society Endangers Our Future*. New York: Norton.

Talen, Ayse Can, Marc A. Weiss, and Sohini Sarkar. 2002. "The Future of Microfinance in the United States: Research, Practice, and Policy Perspectives." In *Replicating Microfinance in the United States*, edited by James H. Carr, Zhong Yi Tong. Washington, DC: Woodrow Wilson Center Press, 331-51.

Taylor, Timothy. 2012. *The Instant Economist: Everything You Need to Know About How the Economy Works*. New York: Plume.

Tough, Paul. 2012. *How Children Succeed: Grit, Curiosity, and the Hidden Power of Character*. Boston: Houghton Mifflin Harcourt.

Wolfram, Catherine, Orie Shelef, and Paul Gertler. 2012. "How Will Energy Demand Develop in the Developing World?" *Journal of Economic Perspectives* 26 (1): 119–38.

Zak, Paul J. and Stephen Knack. 2001. "Trust and Growth." *Economic Journal* 111 (470): 295–321.

Index

About the Authors

Jannett Highfill is professor of economics at Bradley University in Peoria, Illinois. Her research specialty is applied optimal control theory, especially R&D games in intra-industry trade models. Other scholarly interests include urban economics, auction theory, and pedagogy. She has some fifty EconLit articles in such journals as *The Journal of Technology Transfer, Contemporary Economic Policy*, and the *Journal of Urban Economics*. She is past president of the Missouri Valley Economic Association and former editor and editor-in-chief of the *Global Economy Journal*. She has also published two poetry chapbooks, *A Constitution of Silence* and *Light Blessings Drifting Together*, and individual poems in such journals as *The Iowa Review* and *Fifth Wednesday*.

Patricia Podd Webber is retired from many years of teaching economic principles, most recently twenty-five years at Bradley University where she and Jannett became colleagues and friends. She's volunteered for over thirty years at an inner-city agency in Peoria, and for five years at a Saturday "soup kitchen" project feeding 250–400 persons, was a Brownie troop leader in an inner-city neighborhood, and so on. Her undergraduate degree is from Wellesley College and her master's from the University of Illinois, both in economics. Her professional experience includes a stint at the Federal Reserve Bank of Chicago and the Bureau of Economic and Business Research at the University of Illinois. She continues to try to impart family wisdom by example to a growing bevy of grandchildren and their friends.